Scraps & Shirttails II
Continuing the Art of Quilting Green

Bonnie K. Hunter

Scraps & Shirttails II

Continuing the Art of Quilting Green

By Bonnie K. Hunter

Editor: Jenifer Dick
Technical Editor: Christina DeArmond
Book Design: Brian Grubb
Photography: Aaron T. Leimkuehler
Illustration: Eric Sears
Production assistance: Jo Ann Groves

Bonnie K. Hunter
Website: www.quiltville.com • Email: quiltville@gmail.com

Published by Kansas City Star Books
1729 Grand Blvd. • Kansas City, Missouri, USA 64108

First edition, eighth printing · ISBN: 978-1-935362-76-0
Library of Congress Control Number: 2001012345

Printed in the United States of America by
Walsworth, Marceline, MO

To order copies, call StarInfo at **(816) 234-4636** and say "Books."

Kansas City Star Quilts is an imprint of C&T Publishing, Inc.
P.O. Box 1456 Lafayette, CA. 94549 ctpub.com

KANSAS CITY STAR QUILTS
Continuing the Tradition

*The photography in Scraps and Shirttails II took place in the
homes of Jan Rogge, Kansas City, and Brian Grubb also of
Kansas City. Further settings were taken at One Park Place,
luxury condominiums in Kansas City.*

Quilts color my world:
Every piece is a vivid
tone, much like
acrylics or oil paint
on canvas. I surround
myself in tints and
hues and values,
creating every day
art with needle and
thread.

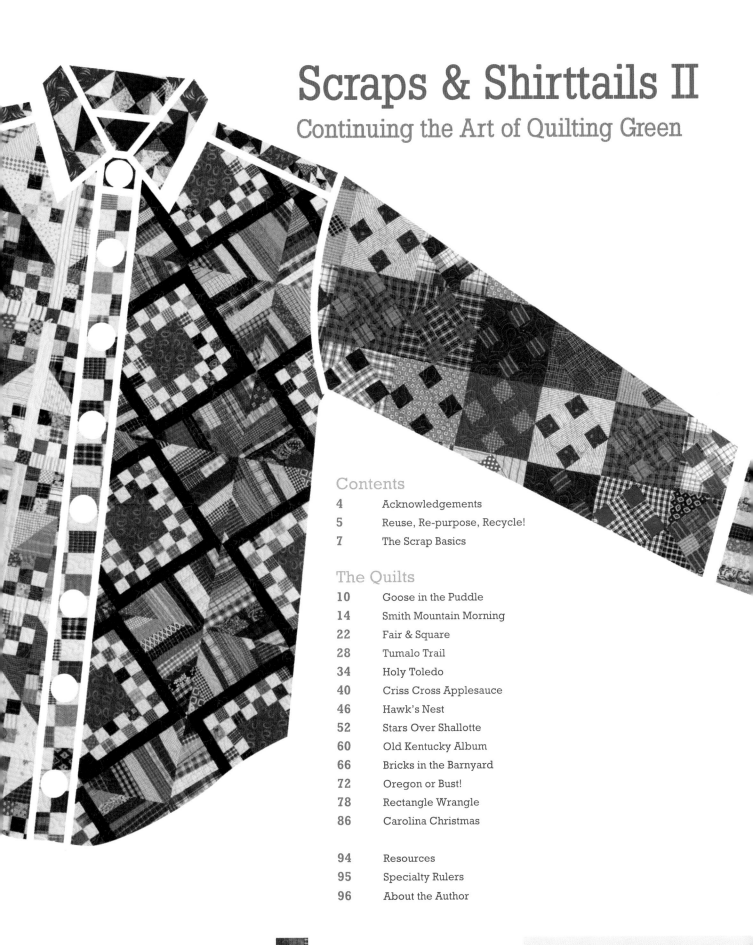

Scraps & Shirttails II
Continuing the Art of Quilting Green

Contents

Foreword

If you've been recycling fabric for fabulous quilts ever since **Scraps & Shirttails** was released in Fall 2008, and you still find your car on autopilot, turning into a Goodwill, the Salvation Army, or flipping an illegal u-turn because of a yard sale sign – in hopes that there just might be the XXXL orange shirt that you need to complete your latest project – this book is for you!

I love the treasure hunting aspect of finding quilting fabric in unexpected places. And that love created a burgeoning overabundance! **Scraps & Shirttails II** grew out of my desire to keep sewing with all that I had found and collected, and from the requests that came from quilters far and wide to design quilts that would also help them use what they had acquired. We are mad for reclaimed and re-purposed fabric and intend to quilt it up!

I also have to thank internet quilter friends far and wide who would do such silly things as fill boxes with "shirt parts" – sleeves, pockets, collars, cuffs and yokes and send them to me, sometimes with no return address attached! What's a scrap quilter to do but find great designs to sew it all up into fun, colorful, useable quilts?

Dedication

This book is dedicated to YOU, the World of Quilters. I wouldn't be doing this without you – the guilds, the bees, the groups of quilters who have been my inspiration for so many of the quilts in this book. I've often said that quilting is not just a hobby, but a lifestyle – something we choose every day to enhance not only our own lives, but the lives of those we love through the gifts of our hands and hearts, our quilts. Quilting is not what we DO, it is who we ARE!

Acknowledgements

Writing acknowledgments can stump me for words more than any other part of writing a book for the simple reason that my life as a quilter and author has been blessed with the help of so many that deserve a mention. This is my third book with Kansas City Star Books, and I don't want to sound like something of a broken record when it comes to thanking those involved in the publishing of **Scraps & Shirttails II**. Nonetheless, each and every one of you deserves my gratitude, and you have it!

Of course, I have to begin – as always – with thanking my immediate family. Dave and I have been married 29 years as I write this. We were married in August of 1981 and have shared quite a life together: Two sons, 10 dogs (at various times, not at once!), at least as many cats, 10 different residences in 5 different states. It's been a whirlwind since the beginning, and I can't imagine experiencing any of it without my family.

My children – Jason and Jeff – are grown now, finding their way into their own lives and I am so proud of the young men they have become and am honored to be their mother. They have been a great support through this whole: "My mom is a Quilter" thing! They "get" me!

My complete and heartfelt thanks go to the staff at Kansas City Star Books for having enough faith in me to tackle this third book. My special thanks go to Doug Weaver and Diane McLendon for taking me on, encouraging me – and especially for Doug who told me over a lunch meeting: "Whatever you are doing, don't stop now!" I promise, Doug – there is no stopping this train.

I'd also like to thank the team that helped put this book together: Brian Grubb, Aaron Leimkuehler, Eric Sears, Christina DeArmond and Jo Ann Groves. Special thanks to Jenifer Dick for agreeing to work with me a third time around as well! She is a very talented quilter herself, and I trust her advice implicitly! Thanks for being a friend, Jenifer!

Remember, if it's still UGLY, you just didn't cut it SMALL ENOUGH!

Bonnie K Hunter

Reuse, Re-purpose, Recycle!

I had a wonderful time writing **Scraps & Shirttails – The Art of Quilting Green** released in 2008. I learned so much from the whole project! I've always been a recycler and it started early on. Some of my first memories as a young child were of going yard sale to yard sale with my mom. Oh, I definitely remember a purple plush stuffed cow named Elsie that was bigger than I was at about 5-years old. I didn't think of yard sales as recycling, but in its own way it was the start of a pattern for my life.

Along with writing that first book came a whole new awareness of all things "green" as I researched how organic cotton is grown and processed, what is happening with corn in the fiber industry, what battings are considered green. I even got to play with new-to-me things like bamboo and how it is used for not only batting, but for fabric! I got to research wool as a natural organic fiber, and at the last minute, rush to include a bit of information on a green batting made from recycled pop bottles.

What I discovered along this journey was that where my heart is, where my head is, and where my quilts are is with that feeling of making do, of using what we already have on hand – be it scraps from yardage or repurposed clothing.

We've heard it over and over: "Use it up – wear it out – make it do, or do without!"

This was a popular slogan in the World War II years, and it stands as true today in this economy as it did then. Take a look around your sewing room. Appreciate your own over-abundance and let's put it to good use!

It all starts with the fabric.

Fabric Selection

Whether store bought or re-purposed, the fabric is the largest part of your quilt. Re-purposing fabric for your scrap quilt starts with fabric collecting. This involves more forethought and planning than searching your favorite quilt shops for the perfect pre-matched fabric line. You need to know where to look, what to look for and how to spot a bargain when you see it. Think of it as a treasure hunt, and be on the lookout!

Here are some logical places to begin your search. As you continue your journey, you'll come up with more sources.

- Thrift shops such as Salvation Army or Goodwill
- Garage and yard Sales, church and school rummage sales – check the newspaper for ads.
- Your friends and family
- Your own closet
- Your stash – always your stash!

When shopping for bargains, look for the largest sizes of men's shirts. There is a lot of fabric in a 3X men's tall, long-sleeved shirt! I figure the shirt back to be larger than a fat quarter. In addition to the back, you get two fronts, two sleeves, cuffs, a collar and pockets making about 1 to 1 1/2 yards of usable fabric per shirt. Compare how much you pay for 1 to 1 1/2 yards of fabric in your area to how much you pay for one gently used shirt. Many times, you'll be getting a true bargain from the shirt – especially if you are in love with the color and the pattern.

There is a lot of fabric in a 3X men's tall, long-sleeved shirt!

And don't forget to check the pajama pants section! There is a lot of fabric in men's XL pajama pants, and some really fun prints. I recently bought a pair that had a well known donut manufacturer's logo and donuts all over it. I KNOW I can't get this licensed fabric off the bolt, and it was sure fun to be able to include it in my growing collection of novelty prints. Travel over to the women's section and look at skirts and dresses too. Then go over to the linens to check the curtains, bed skirts and other items that just might be 100% cotton.

I am always drawn to bold, bright colors and often find that I don't have enough background neutrals on hand. Try really hard to make yourself buy one neutral shirt to go with the other three, four or 12 colored shirts you have in your cart! You need them. Backgrounds are the canvas that your other fabrics will play against. Having a good selection of background neutrals makes the other colors look much better.

That thing called Fabric Content

Yes, it is important. We like fibers that are going to play nicely and give us the result we want. So when I am shopping I am not looking for articles that are heavily worn out. You'd be amazed how many things are on the rack that have not seen a washing machine or have price tags still attached! These must be the obligatory Father's Day, Easter or Christmas shirts that never got worn more than once, if that.

I do read labels just like I would a can of soup at the grocery store. I want to know what the fiber is. There have been times when I have let a really good color go because it had spandex in it. I prefer 100% cotton, but there are a couple of other things I will use that are still natural fibers and give a good result. A cotton/linen blend is still a natural combination and will behave nicely. I also like the texture it gives. A cotton/ramie blend has a feel much like homespun and I have used it with good luck.

In June 2010, I traveled to Minnesota to be with my family for my grandfather's funeral. One evening at my uncle's house, he mentioned that he had some boxes of Grandpa's things and would I be interested? The only thing I wanted was a few of Grandpa's shirts. And I read the labels. Out of all the shirts, only four of them were 100% cotton and they came home with me. I used these shirts in **Criss Cross Applesauce** (found on page 40). Though there were other shirts, I knew these cotton ones would work best with the other shirt fabrics I already had on hand. And since I combine recycled fabrics with my stash and scraps, the 100% cotton means that the shirt fabrics will behave with everything else in my quilts too.

I have had quilters ask me if they can use poly-blend fabrics to make quilts for the grandchildren of loved ones who have passed on. My reply to them is, of course! We can make quilts out of anything, there are no rules there. You just have to know that if you are using poly-blends you are going to have to turn the iron down so you don't melt them. You might have to stabilize them so they don't wiggle so much, and you have to understand that they behave differently than 100% cottons, so the quilt might wear in a different way. But my thoughts, as always are – what is more important to these kids? The memory of Grandpa and being wrapped in quilts made with love from his clothing or the purity of the fiber content? By all means, those kids deserve quilts!

Quilt Backings

Recycling goes BIG on the BACK! It's a great place to include orphan blocks, leftover pieces of fabrics from the front of your quilt, and other fabrics that you may have deemed as too ugly or too out-dated to use on the front of your quilt. I love to do this! Sometimes I'll combine fabrics by color family, cutting them into 10 1/2" squares to piece a back as big as I need it to be. I figure I can get rid of between 6-8 yards of miscellaneous fabrics and fat-quarters by building a back. That's a significant dent in the fabric stash! And of course, that 8 yards used up gives us a free pass to go buy 8 yards of something new!

I'm all about minimizing guilt when it comes to my quilting. I want the old stuff to go so the new stuff can come in guilt free. Be sure to check out the back of **Carolina Christmas** (found on page 93.) It used a large selection of orphan blocks and Christmas prints that just needed a place to blossom. The back is nearly as fun as the front!

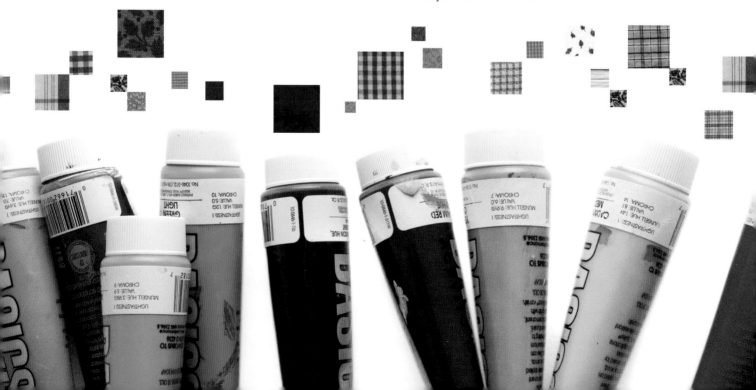

The Scrap Basics

Once you get home from your "Fabric Acquisition Road Trip," throw all your purchases into the wash. I add normal detergent and wash it like my regular laundry. Tumble dry. You don't know the history of these shirts and other items, so washing not only cleans them up, it ensures the fabrics won't bleed once stitched into your quilt.

Cut it up

I find the best tools for deconstructing to be a seam ripper, for quickly removing buttons, and a good pair of sharp dress shears. I save the taking apart event for an evening when I am couch-bound watching a chick flick movie on TV.

Remove the buttons. I save them in a pretty glass jar for decoration. I have dreams of using them to tack a quilt. You can also gift them to someone who collects buttons, and spread the love.

Remove the neck band and collar. Throw the neck band away, saving the collar fabric if there is no stiff interfacing bonded to it. I cut the layers apart on the seam, saving the one piece that is not interfaced.

Remove sleeve cuffs. Cut through all the layers on stitching lines to separate them. Toss the part with the fused interfacing and save the one layer that is not interfaced.

Remove the pockets. The seam ripper will help to get this process started as there is usually triangle backstitching at the upper corners. Collars, cuffs and pockets are the perfect size to cut up for string piecing projects.

Remove the button plackets. I usually just snip and rip these, and toss. There isn't much that can be saved there.

Turn the shirt inside out and simply cut off all the seams and hems. Discard the yoke if it is bonded to interfacing. Often it is a good source for fabric because it is two layers.

Finally, discard ANY parts of the clothing that are too worn to be used.

Pre-cutting and storage

I'm often asked how I get so much quilting accomplished. The answer is easy – organization! By pre-cutting my shirt fabrics and scraps and storing them by size and value – darks and lights – ahead of time, I have the ease of pulling the perfect size so I can just sit and sew. It's a scrap user's dream!

The drawers

Check out your local discount store to see what kind of stackable plastic drawers they have. You can use drawer carts on wheels or free standing stackable drawers. Plastic shoe boxes will work too, but you might find yourself quickly outgrowing them! Just make sure they are clear so you can see what you have in them.

I use the space beneath my longarm quilting machine by stacking my drawers beneath the table side. If you don't have this luxury, think of stacking the drawers against a wall and placing your big-board ironing surface on top of it. There are also bins that will work under beds if your space is limited. The most important thing is to have your strips accessible, and to always be on the lookout for patterns and designs that will help you use what you already have cut and stored!

Once my shirts are cut apart, I keep the shirt backs whole, folded and stored as if they were a fat quarter. I might need them for alternate blocks, sashing or bigger pieces. I pre-cut the shirt fronts, sleeves and other parts into the most popular sizes used in my patterns. Each size goes into its own storage drawer. I pre-cut smaller pieces of stash yardage into the same sizes, too, so the regular scrap stash and the recycled stash can work together.

Strip sizes

I cut fabric pieces that are at least 12" long into 1 1/2", 2", 2 1/2" and 3 1/2" strips, storing them in the plastic drawers by strip width and value, light or dark. For my recycled fabrics, I have four drawers for lights separated by size, and four for darks.

Smaller fabric pieces and shorter strips are cut into squares and bricks by the size of strip:
- 1 1/2" squares and 1 1/2" x 2 1/2" bricks
- 2" squares and 2" x 3 1/2" bricks
- 2 1/2" squares and 2 1/2" x 4 1/2" bricks
- 3 1/2" squares (If bricks are needed I'll cut them from the 3 1/2" strips as needed)

Anything too small or oddly shaped to be cut to a strip width I consider a "string." These also have their own bin.

As you develop your own system, you will discover what sizes you like to work with and incorporate those into your storage drawers as well. Always be on the lookout for how you can use your seemingly unusable scraps and cut them into that size and shape ahead of time. Soon you'll have a sewing room full of organized scraps that are ready to go when you are!

Anything too short to be a strip or a string I consider to be a "crumb." I save those too! I love scrappy paper piecing, and the best thing about paper piecing with small scraps of fabric is that you don't have to rotary cut the scraps down to any particular size. As long as it is big enough to cover that space on the paper foundation, it is big enough to work there.

My crumb bins, string bins, and scrap drawers contain infinite variety! I like to think of my scrap stash as my own personal signature, these are the pieces left from all the quilts I've made throughout the past 30 years. They contain my memories, my history, my life.

Basic Sewing Guidelines

The patterns for the quilts in this book are based on rotary cutting and machine piecing methods. The tools used are also the same as in basic quiltmaking. To avoid frustration, it is necessary to have a sewing machine in good working order. Only a straight stitch is required. There are a few additional tips I've picked up on the way to make my quilt making easier and faster.

That 1/4" seam allowance

It is important to find where the 1/4" seam is on your machine. If you can master this, all your blocks will be the same size and you'll be able to match points perfectly.

There are many ways to set up your machine to sew an accurate 1/4" seam allowance. One of the simplest ways is to use an index card that has 1/4" lines marked on it.

With scissors or your rotary cutter, trim off one end of the index card along one line. The next line on the card should be exactly 1/4" from the edge where you just cut. Slide the index card under the machine presser foot as you would your fabric, and sink the needle into the line. The edge of the card should be 1/4" from the needle. Once you determine where your 1/4" mark is, use masking tape to make a line on your machine bed at that point, and extend it a bit out front of the needle to guide you as you sew.

Now that you've marked your 1/4" and know where it is, flip the index card over and sew on the unlined side, using your tape as a guide. Turn the card back over again and see how close you are to that 1/4" line. Make adjustments with your markings as necessary until you can sew blindly on the back of the card, having your stitching on the line on the front of the card.

Chain piecing with Leaders & Enders

Continuous chain piecing is not a new concept, and I've been doing it for years. By aligning fabric patches, right sides together before sewing, you can feed the fabric pairs through the machine one after another without stopping. This saves your effort and speeds up your quiltmaking, not to mention it saves a ton of thread!

It is through the years, however that I have evolved the process of chain piecing with Leaders & Enders to make, in essence, two quilts at once!

Traditionally a scrap of fabric folded in half is used to start off and finish the line of chain pieced patches. This keeps the thread from bunching up underneath the first patch sewn in the line. But over time, I realized that the little scrap of fabric with its mess of thread was still being thrown away. Now I use pre-cut squares or other shapes as the Leaders & Enders instead of the thread covered scrap. These pieces will become units for another quilt.

Keep a basket of squares by the side of your machine

I find I like to use 2" squares as my favorite size. At the end of a set of chain pieced patches, when it is time to go to the iron and press, match a pair of dark and light squares together and feed it through the machine. Leave this pair under the presser foot and clip the threads behind it. Start a new set of patches to be continuously chain pieced – seeing that your "Ender" has now become your "Leader." Continue until you have several pairs of squares sewn and set to the side of your machine while working on other projects.

Eventually you will have a whole basket of pairs. These pairs can be sewn into four patches, nine patches, or any block you choose. You can also make half-square triangle units this way all while piecing another quilt.

You can learn more about chain piecing with Leaders & Enders in my book, **Adventures with Leaders & Enders.** Ask for it at your local quilt shop or go to Quiltville.com to order.

Pressing

I like to press with a dry iron (no steam). If I feel the area I'm pressing can use the help of steam, I'll spritz it from a water bottle and press. No water is ever poured into my iron. I also find myself doing a lot of finger pressing, and only pressing the block with the iron when it is completed. I've seen expensive irons become "spitty" and ruined by the simple addition of water. Even my cheap irons last years and years because I don't put water in them.

When scrap quilting, it is not always possible to press the seams so that they will oppose the next block in the quilt. It all depends on orientation and how you twist and turn the blocks to create the design with the best arrangement of scraps and colors. In many cases, I find myself re-pressing a seam in the opposite direction before sewing into the final quilt layout. Occasionally a twisted seam requires a GOOD iron pressing! I've also been known to press some bulkier seams open where many patches come together at one point to help eliminate that bulk. I'll do whatever works to get the job done!

Goose
In The Puddle

Inspirations for great quilts are around every corner! In this case, it came in the form of an antique-quilt-turned-cutter found in an Ohio antique mall. A cutter quilt is one that was so well loved during its life that it is nearly worn to shreds, and the only way to preserve what is left is to use the "good parts" to create other items. This booth owner seemed to specialize in household items made from cutter quilts. Everywhere I turned there were toilet seat covers, tank top covers, plunger covers (!!!) and ironing board covers made from old quilts.

In a fit of giggles (for this is not my own personal idea of how to decorate with found quilt parts) I snagged up an ironing board cover with this block design on it. The fabrics in the cutter quilt date from about 1890. I fell in love with the block immediately, and just seeing it worked up into this quilt in recycled fabrics brings to mind the laughter at the other items I'd seen – all in the effort to preserve an old quilt and put it to good use!

This block is also related to the "Goose In The Pond" block, just a bit different, and I was drawn to this difference, hence the name, **"Goose in The Puddle."**

FINISHED BLOCK SIZE: 13"

FINISHED QUILT SIZE: 67" x 83"

PIECING DIAGRAMS ARE FOUND ON PAGE 13.

Fabric requirements

For the blocks and pieced cornerstones
2 yards of assorted blue scraps

1 yard assorted red scraps

3 yards of assorted light/neutral scraps, including vintage-looking shirting prints

For the sashing

1 3/4 yards of red gingham

2 yards of red vintage-looking print

Goose in the Puddle block

Make 20 – 13 1/2" unfinished, finishing at 13".

Each **Goose in the Puddle** block is made of 4 nine-patch units, 12 half-square triangle units and 4 sashing strips and 1 center square.

Nine-patch units

Make 4 – 3 1/2" unfinished, finishing at 3".

From the red scraps, cut:
2 – 1 1/2" x 13" strips

1 – 1 1/2" x 7" strip

From the light/neutral scraps, cut:
1 – 1 1/2" x 13" strips

2 – 1 1/2" x 7" strip

Diagrams are on page 13

A Make Panel 1 (dark/light/dark) using the 7" strips. Press seams toward the red center strip. Sub-cut into 4 – 1 1/2" units. An extra inch in the length of the set is built in for squaring up and trimming.

B Make Panel 2 (light/dark/light) using the 13" strips. Press seams toward the red center strip. Sub-cut into 4 – 1 1/2" units. An extra inch in the length of the set is built in for squaring up and trimming.

C Sew 2 Panel 2 segments to either side of 1 Panel 1 segment. Press. Make 4 nine-patch units per block.

Half-square triangle units

Make 12 – 3 1/2" unfinished, finishing at 3".

From the blue scraps, cut 6 – 3 7/8" squares.

From the light/neutral scraps, cut 6 – 3 7/8" squares.

D Layer the blue squares right sides together with neutral squares and cut on the diagonal from corner to corner to yield 12 half-square triangle pairs. Stitch triangles into half-square triangle units. Press toward blue fabric. Make 12.

Quarter unit

Make 4 – 6 1/2" unfinished, will finish at 6".

E Sew 3 half-square triangle units and 1 nine-patch unit into a four-patch unit as shown in the diagram. Make 4.

Block sashing

From the light/neutral scraps, cut 4 – 1 1/2" x 6 1/2" strips.

From the red scraps, cut 1 – 1 1/2" square.

F Stitch the block together into 3 rows as shown in the diagram, joining the rows to complete the block. Press the seams toward the sashing. Make 20 blocks. Blocks are 13 1/2"unfinished, finishing at 13".

Pieced Sashing

From red gingham, cut 4 – 13 1/2" strips x the width of fabric. Sub-cut into 98 – 1 1/2" x 13 1/2" strips.

From the red print, cut 4 – 13 1/2" strips x the width of fabric. Sub-cut into 49 – 2 1/2" x 13 1/2" strips.

G Stitch a narrow gingham strip to either side of each of the 49 dark red strips. Press seams to the gingham strips.

Pinwheel cornerstones

From the blue scraps, cut 2 – 2 7/8" squares.

From the light/neutral scraps, cut 2 – 2 7/8" squares.

H-I For each cornerstone, match the light squares to the dark squares with right sides together. Cut on the diagonal from corner to corner to yield 4 half-square triangle pairs. Stitch pairs on the diagonal and press toward the blue. Make 4 matching per pin-wheel. Units are 2 1/2" unfinished, finishing at 2"

Arrange the units as shown and sew to complete each pinwheel. Make 30. Pinwheels will measure 4 1/2" unfinished, finishing at 4".

Referring to the Quilt Assembly Diagram on page 13, lay out blocks in 5 rows of 4 blocks each, with rows of sashing and cornerstone pinwheels in between and around the outside edge. Stitch the quilt center in rows, and join the rows to complete the quilt center, pressing seams toward the sashing.

Because the blocks are large, and the sashing is wide, no outer border is needed, but if you want to make the quilt larger, feel free to add borders if desired!

Finishing

I quilted **Goose In The Puddle** with an edge to edge design called "Dandy," designed by Keryn Emmerson of Australia. Turn to the resources on page 94 for contact information.

Binding

I used random 2 1/2" strips of blue for the binding. A perfect finish to a fun quilt with a fun history!

Goose in the Puddle

Directions At-A-Glance

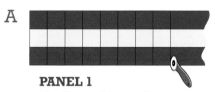

PANEL 1
Cut 8 matching units
per block, 200 total

PANEL 2
Cut 4
matching units per
block, 100 total

NINE-PATCH UNIT
3 1/2" unfinished
Make 4 matching per
block, 80 total

**HALF-SQUARE
TRIANGLE UNIT**
3 1/2" unfinished
Make 12 matching
per block, 240 total

QUARTER UNIT
Make 4 matching
per block, 80 total

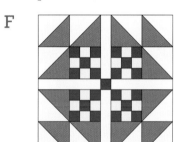

**GOOSE IN THE
PUDDLE BLOCK**
13 1/2" unfinished
Make 20

SASHING
13 1/2" x 3 1/2" unfinished
Make 49

**PINWHEEL
UNITS**
2 1/2" unfinished
Make 4 matching
per block,
120 total

**PINWHEEL
CORNERSTONE**
4 1/2" unfinished
Make 30

ASSEMBLY DIAGRAM

14

Smith Mountain Morning

In May 2010 I had the privilege of teaching for the Virginia Consortium of Quilters in Smith Mountain Lake, Virginia. Spring was in full bloom and the surroundings were just breathtaking. Early morning sunrises over the beautiful Blue Ridge Mountains inspired the name for this pattern, capturing the wonderful memories forever in my mind.

True to the traditions of ages gone by, this design uses scraps of unbleached muslin in a variety of dye lots. Muslin is the perfect accompaniment to recycled plaids, stripes and prints. A bonus bag of brown calicoes dating back to the 1980s and 1990s gifted to me at a trunk show in Marietta, Georgia also played its part in completing the medley of repurposed scraps.

Smith Mountain Morning is a two-block quilt, with the star block, a 54-40 or Fight variation, in two colorways, and a Chimney and Cornerstones log cabin variation which is rotated to complete the design between the stars.

FINISHED BLOCK SIZE: 9"

FINISHED QUILT SIZE: 71" x 80"

PIECING DIAGRAMS ARE FOUND ON PAGE 19.

Fabric requirements

For the blocks and outer border

3 yards of assorted blue scraps

3 yards of assorted brown scraps

3 yards of unbleached muslin

For the inner border

1/2 yard of light blue

Star blocks

Make 16 blue and 12 brown – 9 1/2" unfinished, finishing at 9"

The Star blocks are made in two colorways, blue and brown. Each are made of 4 star point units, 4 half-square triangle units and 1 center pinwheel unit.

I used my Tri Recs rulers and 3 1/2" strips to make the star points for this block. Templates are provided for those who do not have access to this ruler. The Easy Angle ruler was used with 3 1/2" strips and 2" strips for the two sizes of half-square triangles in this quilt. The Companion Angle ruler and 2" strips were used for the quarter-square units in the center of the Chimney & Cornerstone blocks. Please see the section on specialty rulers on page 94 for more info on using this method.

Hint: Remember to cut the star points mirror image so there is one left star point and one right star point for either side of the base triangle.

Star points

From the muslin, cut:
112 triangles using Template A

From the blue, cut:
64 star point triangles using Template B

64 star point triangles using Template C

From the brown, cut:
48 star point triangles using Template B

48 star point triangles using Template C

Templates are found on page 21.

Diagrams are found on
page 19-20

Star Points continued.

A Stitch 1 Template B and C
triangle to either side of the Template
A triangle. Press to the dark. Make 64
blue and 48 brown. Units are 3 1/2"
unfinished, finishing at 3".

Center pinwheels

From the blue scraps, cut 56 –
2 3/8" squares.

From the brown scraps, cut 56 –
2 3/8" squares.

B Match blue squares with brown
squares with right sides together and
slice once on the diagonal from corner
to corner to yield 112 half square
triangle pairs. Stitch, press to the dark
and trim dog ears. Make 112. Units are
2" unfinished.

C Arrange triangles as shown in
diagram and sew. Make 28
pinwheel centers. Units are 3 1/2"
unfinished, finishing at 3".

Corner triangles

From the muslin,
cut 56 – 3 7/8" squares.

From the brown scraps,
cut 32 – 3 7/8" squares.

From the blue scraps,
cut 24 – 3 7/8" squares.

D Match blue and brown squares
with muslin squares, right sides
together, and slice on the diagonal
from corner to corner to yield 112
half-square triangle units. Stitch, press
to the dark and trim dog ears. Make
64 brown and 48 blue. Units are 3 1/2"
unfinished, finishing at 3".

Block assembly

E-F Arrange pieces as shown for 16 blue stars with brown corners, and 12 brown stars with blue corners. Stitch block into rows, and sew rows together and press to complete each block.

Chimney and Cornerstones block

Make 28 – 9 1/2" unfinished, finishing at 9".

The Chimney and Cornerstone blocks are made similar to a log cabin block. Each requires a quarter-square unit for the center surrounded by strips and cornerstones for the logs.

Center quarter-square traingles

From the blue scraps, cut 28 – 4 1/4" squares.

From the brown scraps, cut 28 – 4 1/4" squares.

Lay blue and brown squares right sides together and cut on the diagonal twice with an X to yield 112 matched quarter-square triangle pairs.

Hint: When sewing these, you will want to keep the same color on top as they feed through the machine so colors will fall in the right places when quarter square units are sewn together.

G Sew pairs. Press seam toward brown triangles. Trim dog ears. Match unit halves together to complete the quarter-square centers. Make 28. Units are 3 1/2" unfinished, finishing at 3".

Logs

From the brown, cut:

56 – 1 1/2" x 3 1/2" rectangles
56 – 1 1/2" x 5 1/2" rectangles
56 – 1 1/2" x 7 1/2" rectangles

From the blue, cut:

56 – 1 1/2" x 3 1/2" rectangles
56 – 1 1/2" x 5 1/2" rectangles
56 – 1 1/2" x 7 1/2" rectangles

From the muslin, cut:

336 – 1 1/2" squares

Stitch 1 muslin square to each end of the blue rectangles. Press to the blue.

Note: 1 1/2" strips of muslin can be sewn to the 3 1/2", 5 1/2" and 7 1/2" widths of blue fabric before sub-cutting them into the 1 1/2" logs. Because I was using 1 1/2" pre-cut scrap strips to piece this quilt, I chose to do it the old fashioned way.

H Sew 2 brown 3 1/2" logs to either side of the 28 quarter-square triangle units. Press seams to the brown logs.

I Sew the 3 1/2" blue logs with cornerstones to the top and bottom of the unit to complete Round One. Press seams to the blue logs.

J Sew the 5 1/2" brown logs to the sides of the unit. Press toward the logs just added.

K Add the 5 1/2" blue logs with the cornerstones to the top and bottom of the unit to complete Round Two. Press seams toward the blue logs.

L Sew the 7 1/2" brown logs to the sides of the unit. Press toward the logs just added.

M Complete the Chimney and Cornerstone blocks by adding the remaining 7 1/2" blue logs with cornerstones to the top and bottom of the unit. Press seams toward the blue logs just added. Make 28. Blocks are 9 1/2" unfinished, finishing at 9".

Quilt top center assembly

Lay out blocks as shown in the Quilt Assembly Diagram, alternating the rows of brown stars and blue stars as shown in the diagram. Rotate the Chimney and Cornerstone blocks to complete the rounds around each star block. Sew the blocks into rows, and join the rows to complete the quilt center. Press.

Borders
Inner border

From the light blue, cut 8 – 2" strips x the width of fabric.

Join the strips end to end with diagonal seams into one long length, measuring approximately 320" long. Press seams open.

Lay quilt out on the floor, smoothing it gently. Do not tug or pull. Measure the quilt through the center from top to bottom. Cut two inner side borders this length. Sew inner side borders to the quilt sides with right sides together, pinning to match centers and ends. Ease where necessary to fit. Press seams to the borders.

Repeat for top and bottom inner borders, measuring across the quilt center, including the borders just added in the measurement. Cut top and bottom inner borders this length. Stitch top and bottom inner borders to quilt center, pinning to match centers and ends, easing where necessary. Press seams to borders.

Pieced outer border

From the muslin, cut: 94 triangles using Template A

From brown scraps, cut:
94 star point triangles using Template B

From blue scraps, cut:
94 star point triangles using Template C

N Stitch 1 Template B and C triangle to either side of the Template A triangle. Make sure B is always on the left. Press to the dark. Make 94. Units are 3 1/2" unfinished.

Border Corner units

From the brown, cut 2 – 3 7/8" squares.

From the muslin, cut 2 – 3 7/8" squares.

O Match muslin squares to brown squares with right sides together and cut once on the diagonal from corner to corner, to yield 4 triangle pairs. Stitch. Press and trim dog ears. Make 4. Units are 3 1/2" unfinished, finishing at 3"

Side borders

P Join 25 units end to end as shown. Press. Make 2. Attach to the quilt sides, pinning to match ends and centers, easing where necessary to fit. Press to the inner striped border.

Top and bottom borders

Q Join 22 units end to end. Attach 1 brown half square triangle unit to each end of both the top and bottom borders. Make 2. Attach top and bottom borders to quilt, pinning to match ends and centers, easing where necessary to fit. Press seams to inner striped border.

Finishing

Smith Mountain Morning is quilted with a sand colored thread in a pattern called Je T'aime by Urban Elemetz. Turn to the resources on page 94 for contact information.

The quilt is bound in a dark tan check to finish.

On the flip side *(shown left)*

I had the perfect tan plaid – just not enough of it! A quick dig through a box of leftover units uncovered a small pile of blocks remaining from a previous quilt. I simply stitched the units together, inserted them between two widths of my tan plaid backing fabric and made the backing big enough. It doesn't matter to me that the units on the back have nothing to do with the fabrics on the front!

Smith Mountain Morning

Directions At-A-Glance

A

B

D

E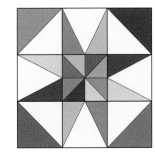

A) STAR POINTS
3 1/2" unfinished
Make 64 blue
Make 48 brown

B) PINWHEEL UNITS
2" unfinished
Make 112

CORNER TRIANGLES
3 1/2" unfinished
Make 48 blue
Make 64 brown

BLUE STAR
9 1/2" unfinished
Make 16

C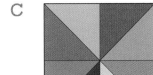

STAR CENTER PINWHEEL
3 1/2" unfinished
Make 28

F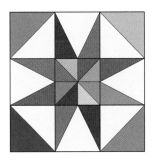

BROWN STAR
9 1/2" unfinished
Make 12

G

CENTER QUARTER-SQUARE TRIANGLE
3 1/2" unfinished
Make 28

H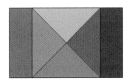

M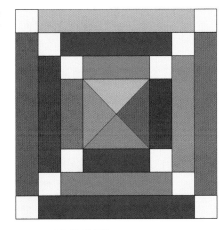

I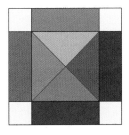

J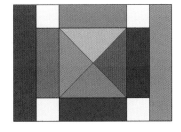

CHIMNEY AND CORNERSTONE BLOCK
9 1/2" unfinished
Make 28

K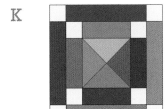

L

N

O

P

BORDER UNIT
3 1/2" unfinished
Make 94

BORDER CORNER UNIT
3 1/2" unfinished
Make 4

SIDE BORDERS • Make 2

Q

ASSEMBLY DIAGRAM

TOP AND BOTTOM BORDERS

Templates

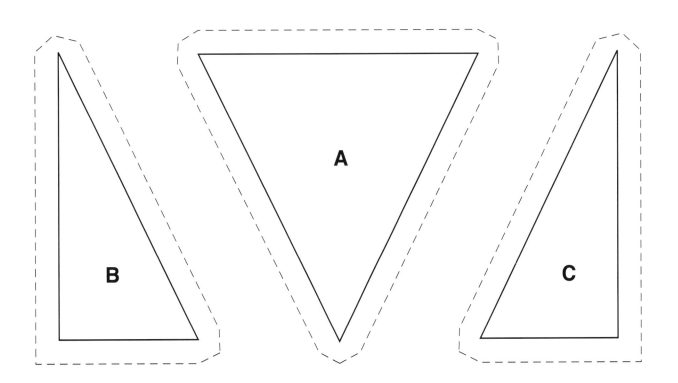

B

A

C

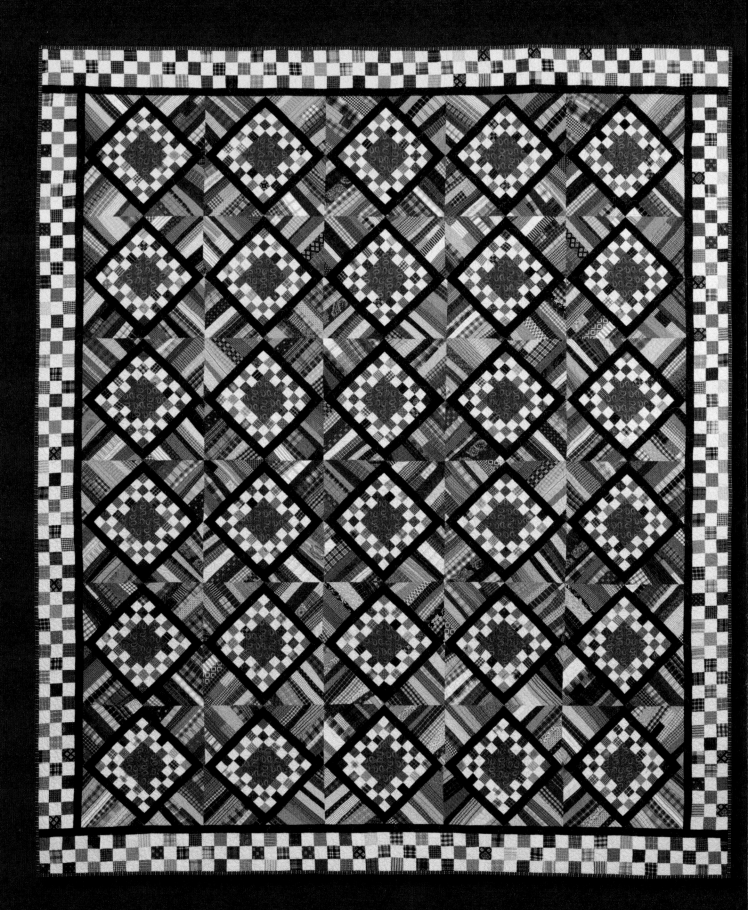

Fair & Square

When I think of those quilters of yesterday, I can imagine myself then, saving every last bit for use in a quilt somewhere. In a world of "disposable everything" I find myself saving even the smallest bits and dreaming, plotting and planning of where I could use each little piece.

This quilt is the perfect example of using various elements of my own scraps to pull together a quilt that sings! The string blocks are stitched from the saved bits of decon-structed clothing for use in quilt making: collars, cuffs, pockets, plackets – all the "too small to be a real strip" pieces that I still could not bear to toss away. The smallest checkerboards surrounding the red squares are 1 1/2" squares of recycled scraps and squares of muslin,

The two sizes of checkerboard border were pieced from strips of recycled fabrics and muslin in speedy strip pieced fashion,

FINISHED BLOCK SIZE: 10"

FINISHED QUILT SIZE: 81 1/2" x 96"

PIECING DIAGRAMS ARE FOUND ON PAGE 26-27

Fabric requirements

For the checkerboard blocks and border

3 yards unbleached muslin

2 1/2 yards assorted scraps

2/3 yard of red print

1/2 yard of light blue

For the checkerboard block sashing and inner border

2 yards black

For the alternate block and setting triangles

5 yards assorted string scraps

For the foundation piecing

Newsprint, tracing paper or phone book pages

Checkerboard blocks

Make 30 – 10 1/2" unfinished blocks

Each Checkerboard block is made of 12 four-patch units, a center square and 4 sashing strips.

Four-patch units

Make 360 – 12 per block – 2 1/2" unfinished, finishing at 2".

From the assorted scraps, cut 720 – 1 1/2" squares.

From the muslin, cut 720 – 1 1/2" squares.

Diagrams are found on page 26-27

A Sew a dark and muslin square together. Press to the dark. Make 720 units. Sew these units to make the finished four-patch units. Make 360. Units measure 2 1/2" unfinished, finishing at 2".

As I made my four-patch units, I pinned them in bundles of 10 so it was easy for me to count how many I had.

Note: If you choose to strip piece the blocks, cut the assorted scraps and muslin into 1 1/2" strips. Since the length of yo ur scrap strips determines the number of units you can get from them, no exact number of strips to cut is given. Piece the dark to the muslin and press to the dark. Sub-cut into 720 – 1 1/2" units. Sew together to make 360 four-patch blocks.

Center square

From the red print, cut 30 – 4 1/2" squares.

B For each block, join 2 four-patch units side-by-side paying attention to the placement of lights and darks as shown in the diagram. Sew to either side of the red center square. Press to the center square.

C Lay out the four-patch units to form the top and bottom row of the checkerboard, watching placement of lights and darks. Join these together, and add to block center top and bottom. Press to the center square. Make 30. Units are 8 1/2" unfinished, finishing at 8".

Block sashing

From solid black, cut:

60 – 1 1/2" x 8 1/2" rectangles.

60 – 1 1/2" x 10 1/2" rectangles.

D Stitch the two short, black strips to the block sides. Press to the sashing. Stitch the remaining 2 strips to block top and bottom. Press to the sashing. Make 30. Blocks are 10 1/2" unfinished, finishing at 10".

Alternate blocks, half blocks and corner triangles

Make 20 – 10 1/2" unfinished

Make 18 half blocks

Make 4 corner triangles

Though it looks like a straight set quilt, this is an on-point quilt with half string blocks as setting triangles. I originally thought of turning the checkerboard blocks on point using the string blocks as triangles, but this left bias all on the outside edges and was a bit unwieldy to deal with so doing it this way just assembled so much nicer for me.

From newsprint, tracing paper or phone book pages, cut: 60 – 8 1/2"" squares to be used as a foundation for string piecing.

E The strings can be any width of fabric from 3/4" to 2 1/4" inches wide. Strings can taper from wide to narrow for interest, and short strings can be seamed together end to end to make a piece big enough to cover its place on the foundation.

When string piecing, shorten your stitch length to 18-20 stitches per inch and use a larger needle such as a size 90/14 denim needle to make it easy to remove the foundation when done. I remove the paper after piecing each block to eliminate the extra bulk at the seams when joining the blocks together.

Start by laying two strips right sides together across the center diagonal of the foundation square. Sew the two pieces together through the paper. Flip the top strip over and press. Continue adding strips until the entire foundation is covered.

String Piecing   **String-Pieced Unit Before Squaring Up**

Hint: I like to have two blocks going at one time. Feed one block through the machine and without cutting the threads, feed the second block through. Clip the first block off the chain of thread behind the presser foot and without removing the second block from underneath the machine foot, bring the first block forward and add another piece to it. You can string piece continuously this way without any messy long threads all over your sewing area.

Repeat to make 60 string blocks. Trim blocks to 8 1/2" square. Lay your ruler across the block from corner to corner as shown and cut all of the blocks on the diagonal to yield 120 string triangles. At this point, carefully remove paper.

F Mix and match the string triangles in sets of 4 to arrange 20 alternate blocks. Sew together and press seams to one side. Square these up to 10 1/2" unfinished, finishing at 10".

G-H Sew 18 pairs of triangles together to make 18 half blocks. These will float the quilt a bit, and will be trimmed down after the quilt is assembled. The 4 remaining triangles are the corner triangles.

Quilt top center assembly

Referring to the Quilt Assembly Diagram on page 27, lay out the blocks and setting squares, filling in the sides with the setting triangles and corners. I like to piece diagonally set quilts into two halves. This keeps things from being too unwieldy, especially when sewing a large quilt top. Join quilt top halves to complete quilt center.

Trim the quilt center, leaving 1/4" seam allowance beyond the black sashing around the outside edge of the top. Stay stitch around the edge by setting the machine at a large stitch length and stitching just inside of that 1/4" measurement. This will help keep the strings from coming unstitched, and add some stability to that bias edge.

Borders

Outer checkerboard border

The checkerboard border is made with 2" strips and finishes at 4 1/2" wide. This quilt was such a great way to use up various chunks and hunks of muslin left from projects of long ago! I didn't even pay attention to make sure everything was the same dye lot. Any difference in the shading adds charm and character!

From the scraps, cut 2" wide strips.

From the muslin, cut 2" wide strips.

I-J Sew strip sets of dark-light-dark to make Panel 1 and light-dark-light to make Panel 2. Press to the dark strips. Sub-cut into 2"

units. Sew one long border length, alternating the 1 and 2 units, until you reach a length of approximately 360", pressing as you go.

Note: The number of sub-cuts you can get from each strip set depends on the length of your scrap strip. I didn't count when making this quilt how many units I needed. In fact, I just kept piecing and piecing until I had way more than I needed and ended up using the leftover checkered border length on the back of the quilt just to use it up!

Inner black border

From the black, cut 9 – 1 1/2" strips x the width of fabric.

Join the strips end to end on the diagonal to make about a 360" long strip. Press seams open. Stitch the black inner border down the full length of the checkerboard border. Press seams to the black border.

Lay out the quilt center, and measure down the center, from top to bottom. Cut two lengths from the pieced border this measurement. Yes, you may be cutting squares in half, and that's okay!

Stitch the border to the quilt sides, pinning to match centers and ends and easing where necessary. Press seam to the black inner border.

Measure the quilt again across the center from side to side, including the borders just added in that measurement. Cut the top and bottom borders to this length. Attach to top and bottom of quilt by pinning to match centers and ends and easing where necessary. Press seams to the black inner border.

Finishing

Fair and Square is quilted in an antique gold thread using a design by Urban Elementz called Harvest Winds. Turn to the resources page for contact information.

The quilt is bound in a red stripe that ties the red and black elements of the quilt together.

On the flip side *(shown right)*

I used the leftover checkerboard in piecing the back out of random lengths of red yardage that just needed to leave my shelves! What a great way to clear out some fabric that had been sitting there unused for far too long. My favorite justification? If I can clear out 7 yards of old stuff for the back of a quilt, it gives me a free pass to go buy 7 yards of something NEW!

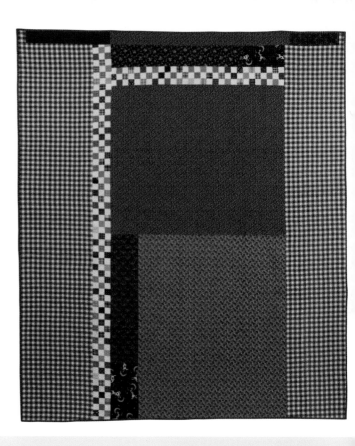

Fair & Square   Directions At-A-Glance

A

FOUR-PATCH UNIT
2 1/2" unfinished
Make 360

B

C

D

CHECKERBOARD BLOCK
10 1/2" unfinished
Make 30

E

STRING BLOCKS
9" unfinished -
Make 60
Cut in half on the
diagonal to make
120 String Triangles

F

ALTERNATE BLOCK
10 1/2" unfinished -
Make 20

G

HALF BLOCK
Make 18

H

CORNER TRIANGLE
Make 4

I

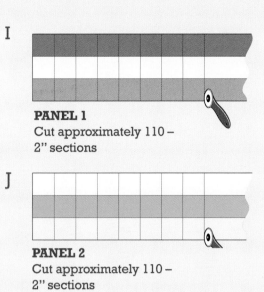

PANEL 1
Cut approximately 110 –
2" sections

J

PANEL 2
Cut approximately 110 –
2" sections

**ASSEMBLY
DIAGRAM**

Tumalo Trail

A suitcase full of recycled shirt fabrics in light and dark, a big zippered bag of really OLD 1 1/2" strips, a circle of five friends sewing together for a whole week and capping off our time together with a visit to the quilt show in Sister's Oregon? Priceless!

I had a few test blocks made before arriving, but quickly set to work to power sew this top together. The objective? Get RID of those 1 1/2" strips that had been languishing, some of them dating back to my early quilting years. The piano key border was quite hilarious, I just kept sewing and sewing and sewing, and by the time I was done, I think I had enough border to go around this quilt three times! Needless to say, there will be more piano key borders showing up on future quilts!

FINISHED BLOCK SIZE: 9"
FINISHED QUILT SIZE: 72 1/2" x 82 1/2"
PIECING DIAGRAMS ARE FOUND
ON PAGES 32-33.

Fabric requirements

For blocks and outer border
4 yards of assorted light scraps
4 yards of assorted dark scraps

For cornerstones
1/4 yard assorted blue scraps

For inner border
3/4 yard of assorted red scraps

Tumalo Trail blocks

Make 42 – 9 1/2" unfinished, finishing at 9".
This block is made of 5 nine-patch units and 4 half-square triangle units.

Nine-patch units

From the light scraps, cut lengths into 1 1/2" wide strips.

From the dark scraps, cut lengths into 1 1/2" wide strips.

Because we are working with 1 1/2" wide scrap strips in light and dark, and all strip lengths will vary, you will need to make as many strip sets as you need to get the number of units required.

Diagrams are on pages 32-33

Strip Set A

A Sew 2 dark strips on either side of 1 light strip. Press to the outside strips. Sew as many strip sets as you need to sub-cut into 420 – 1 1/2" sections.

Note: You will want to cut your strips from as many different colors and prints as you can to keep it scrappy!

Strip Set B

B Sew 2 light strips on either side of 1 dark strip. Press to the center strip. Sew as many strip sets as you need to sub-cut into 210 – 1 1/2" sections.

C Combine the units to stitch 210 scrappy nine-patch units.

Quilt top assembly

From the light scraps,
cut 97 – 1 1/2" x 9 1/2" strips for sashing.

From the blue scraps,
cut 56 – 1 1/2" squares for cornerstones.

Referring to the quilt assembly diagram lay out the blocks in rows along with the sashing pieces and the cornerstones. Stitch the quilt center into rows, pressing seams toward the sashing, and away from the cornerstones. Join the rows to complete quilt center.

Half-square triangle units

Make 42 sets of 4 matching units - 3 1/2" unfinished

I used my easy angle ruler and 3 1/2" strips to make the half square triangles for this block. The traditional method of using 3 7/8" squares is given for those who do not have access to this ruler. Please view section on specialty rulers for more info on using this method. You can use any method that gives you a 3" finished half square triangle unit.

Each block contains 4 identical half-square triangle units, but each block is different from the next.

From the light fabric, cut 2 – 3 7/8" squares.

From the dark fabric, cut 2 – 3 7/8" squares.

D Place dark squares on top of light squares with right sides together and slice once on the diagonal to yield 4 half-square triangle pairs. Stitch. Press to the dark. Trim dog ears. Make 42.

E Layout block as shown in the diagram. Stitch block units into rows and join rows to complete block. Press. Make 42.

Borders
Inner border

Cut the assorted red scraps into 1 1/2" strips. Join them end to end with diagonal seams to make a strip approximately 280" long.

Lay the quilt out on the floor, smoothing it gently. Do not tug or pull. Measure the quilt through the center from top to bottom. Cut two inner side borders this length. Sew inner side borders to the quilt sides with right sides together, pinning to match centers and ends. Ease where necessary to fit. Press seams to the borders.

Repeat for top and bottom inner borders, measuring across the quilt center, including the borders just added in the measurement. Cut top and bottom inner borders this length. Stitch top and bottom inner borders to quilt center, pinning to match centers and ends, easing where necessary.

Press seams to the borders.

Piano key border

F Cut random scraps into 1 1/2" strips. Sew together into pairs, and join pairs into panels of 4. Press seams to one side. Sub-cut the border panels into 5" units. Join units side-by-side arranging scrap colors in a pleasing manner. You will need about 360" of piano key border.

Border Corners

Though the quilt looks like the quilt has mitered corners, it doesn't!

If you are using the Easy Angle ruler:

Place two lengths of border with right sides facing. Using the easy angle ruler, cut 4 triangle pairs using the 5" marking on the ruler. Stitch. Press. Corner units will measure 5" unfinished, the same width as your border.

Note: There is sufficient length in the piano key border if you use the Easy Angle.

If you are sewing without the Easy Angle ruler:

G Cut about 24-26 random strips 1 1/2" x 6". Join them side-by-side to make a length measuring approximately 24" long. Press. Cut into 4 - 6" squares.

Place squares right sides together (with stripes facing the same direction) and slice on the diagonal to yield 4 triangle pairs. Stitch pairs into 4 corner units. Trim to 5" square.

H *Note:* The strips are not intended to meet at the center seam to add variety and character! Make 4 border corners.

Lay out the quilt top and measure from top to bottom through the center including red border just added. Cut two side borders from the piano key border this length. Measure side to side through the quilt center including he red inner border and cut a top and bottom border this length.

Add the side borders to the quilt center, pinning to match centers and ends. Stitch. Press to the inner red borders. Add the mitered corner squares to each end of the top and bottom borders and stitch these to the quilt center, pinning to match centers and ends. Press to the inner red borders.

After borders are added, set the machine at a bit longer stitch length, and stay stitch around the outside edge of the quilt top to prevent any seams from opening as the quilt is handled in the quilting process.

Finishing

Tumalo Trail is quilted in a tan thread using an edge to edge designed by Darlene Epp called Paisley. Turn to the resources on page 94 for contact information.

The quilt is finished off in a black binding.

Tumalo Trail
Directions At-A-Glance

A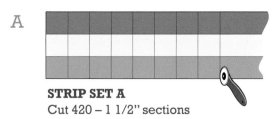

STRIP SET A
Cut 420 – 1 1/2" sections

B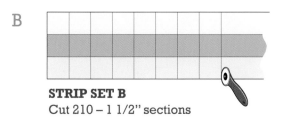

STRIP SET B
Cut 210 – 1 1/2" sections

C  D

NINE-PATCH UNIT
Make 210
3 1/2" unfinished

HALF-SQUARE TRIANGLE UNIT
Make 42 sets of matching units, 4 per block
3 1/2" unfinished

E

TUMALO TRAIL
9 1/2" unfinished
Make 42

F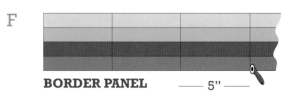

BORDER PANEL ___ 5" ___

G
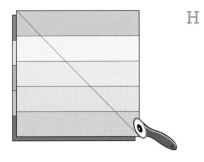

H
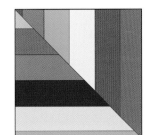

G) BORDER CORNER
6" unfinished

H) CORNER BLOCK
Make 4 - 5" unfinished

ASSEMBLY DIAGRAM

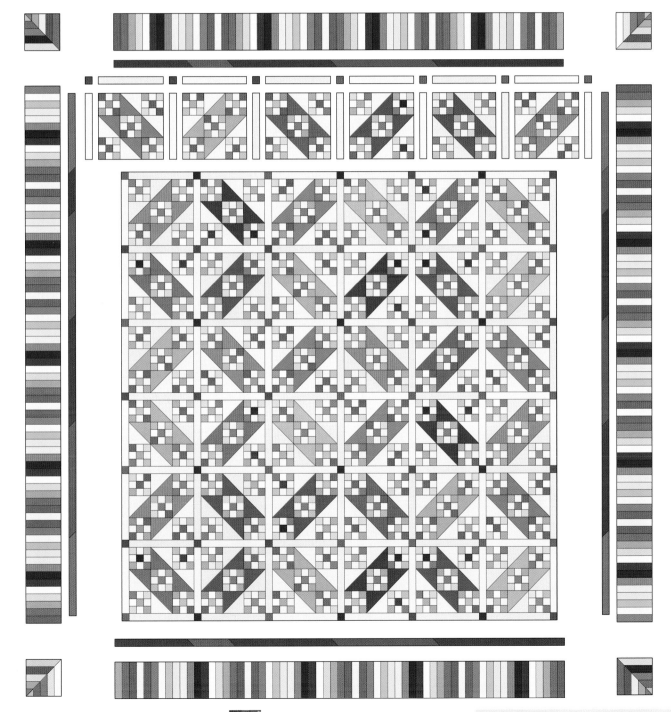

Holy Toledo

Summer of 2009. I had the best time staying with my quilter-friend, Janice while visiting several guilds in Ohio. I'd go do my thing for the day, come back to her house as my 'home base' and we'd sew some more. It was like our own personal retreat in between teaching classes. The large triangles in this top were actually rejected setting triangles from another top, also in this book! Discarded setting squares became the perfect starting point for the Holy Toledo blocks, which remind me of basket blocks minus the basket feet! Similar to a Lady of the Lake block, try twisting and turning these to see the many lay outs that are possible! I do love this layout, which reminds me of giant quilting thread spools.

I used my Easy Angle ruler and 2 1/2" strips and 6 1/2" strips to make the half-square triangles for this quilt. The traditional method of cutting squares is given for those who don't have access to this ruler. See page 95 for more on specialty rulers.

FINISHED BLOCK SIZE: 8"
FINISHED QUILT SIZE: 76"x 92"
PIECING DIAGRAMS ARE FOUND
ON PAGES 38-39.

Fabric requirements

For the blocks and outer pieced border

4 1/4 yards assorted dark scraps

4 1/4 yards assorted light scraps

For inner border

3/4 yard cream shirting stripe

Holy Toledo blocks

Make 80 – 8 1/2" unfinished, finishing at 8"
Each Holy Toledo block is made of 1 large half-square triangle unit and 7 small half-square triangle units.

Large half-square triangle units

Make 80 – 6 1/2" unfinished, finishing at 6"

From the dark scraps, cut 40 – 6 7/8" squares.

From the light scraps, cut 40 – 6 7/8" squares.

Diagrams are on pages 38-39

A Match light squares to dark squares with right sides together, and slice from corner to corner on the diagonal, yielding 80 triangle pairs. Stitch these with a 1/4" seam allowance and press to the dark. Trim dog ears. Make 80. Units measure 6 1/2" unfinished.

Small half-square triangles units

Make 560 – 2 1/2" unfinished, finishing at 2"

From the dark scraps, cut 280 – 2 7/8" squares

From the light scraps, cut 280 – 2 7/8" squares

B Match light squares to dark squares with right sides together, and slice from corner to corner on the diagonal, yielding 560 triangle pairs. Stitch these with a 1/4" seam allowance and press to the dark. Trim dog ears. Make 560. Units measure 2 1/2" unfinished.

C Match 3 random small triangle units together with darks positioned as shown and sew. Make 80.

D Match 4 random small triangle units together with darks pointed as shown and sew. It can be tricky to be sure the triangles face the right way! Make 80.

E Join the block side triangles as shown to light side of large half-square triangle unit. Press to the large half-square triangle unit. Add block bottom triangles to complete the block. Press to the large half-square triangle unit. Make 80. Blocks are 8 1/2" unfinished, finishing at 8".

Quilt top assembly

Referring to the Quilt Assembly Diagram, lay out the blocks 8 across and 10 down, twisting and turning them to find your correct placement. Sew the blocks into rows, and join the rows to complete the quilt top center. Press.

Inner border

From the cream shirting stripe, cut 8 – 2 1/2" strips x the width of fabric.

Join the strips end to end with diagonal seams to create one long length, measuring approximately 320". Press the seams open.

Lay quilt out on the floor, smoothing it gently. Do not tug or pull. Measure the quilt through the center from top to bottom. Cut two inner side borders this length. Sew inner side borders to the quilt sides with right sides together, pinning to match centers and ends. Ease where necessary to fit. Press seams to the borders.

Repeat for top and bottom inner borders, measuring across the quilt center, including the borders just added in the measurement. Stitch top and bottom inner borders to quilt center, pinning to match centers and ends, easing where necessary. Press seams to the borders.

Pieced outer border

F While the center blocks have scrappy triangles with no rhyme or reason to placement, some order comes into play in the outer border. Each of the 32 border sections is made of 8 identical half-square triangle units.

To make 1 border unit, cut:

4 – 2 7/8" squares from the same dark scraps

4 – 2 7/8" squares from the same light scraps

Match 4 dark squares to 4 light squares with right-sides together. Slice the squares on the diagonal from corner to corner to yield 8 half square triangle pairs. Sew pairs together. Press. Make 8. Units measure 2 1/2", finishing at 2".

Lay out the squares as shown in the diagram and sew to complete 1 border unit. Make 36 in assorted light/dark color combinations.

Corner pinwheel unit

Study the quilt diagram to see how the triangles turn the corner. Two triangles will be sewn to the end of each side borders, and 2 to the end of each top and bottom border. The corner unit itself is a pinwheel. The pinwheels and connectors can be a different color for each corner, but you will need 8 of the same half-square triangles to complete each unit.

To make 1 pinwheel and 2 half pinwheel units, cut:

4 – 2 7/8" squares from the same dark scraps

4 – 2 7/8" squares from the same light scraps

G Referring to the diagram, sew 1 pinwheel block. Make 4 in assorted light/dark color combinations.

H Referring to the diagram, sew 2 half pinwheel units. Make 8 in assorted light/dark color combinations to match the pinwheel blocks.

Side borders

Join 10 border units end to end for each side border. Add a half pin-wheel to match the desired corner pinwheel at the end of each border, following the light/dark pattern of the border. Watch the diagram to be sure triangles are turning the right direction. Press. Add the side borders to the quilt with right sides together. Press seams to the inner border.

Top and bottom borders

Join 8 border units end to end for each top and bottom border. Add a half pinwheel to match each corner pinwheel to each end of top and bottom border. I find it helpful to lay out the whole quilt at this point to make sure the units are where I want them to be. Add the pinwheel corners to each end of the top and bottom borders. Press. Sew borders to the top and bottom of quilt center to complete the top. Press.

Finishing

Holy Toledo is quilted in a sand colored thread with a pattern called Moon Flower, designed by Keryn Emmerson of Australia. Refer to the resources page for contact information.

Binding

I bound **Holy Toledo** in a medium blue vintage looking stripe that emphasized the blue shirt fabrics in the quilt center.

A

LARGE HALF-SQUARE TRIANGLE UNIT
6 1/2" unfinished
Make 80 in assorted light/dark color combinations

B

SMALL HALF-SQUARE TRIANGLE UNIT
2 1/2" unfinished
Make 560 in assorted light/dark color combinations

C

BLOCK SIDE TRIANGLES
Make 80

D

BLOCK BOTTOM TRIANGLES
Make 80

E

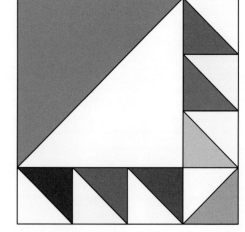

HOLY TOLEDO BLOCK
8 1/2" unfinished • Make 80

F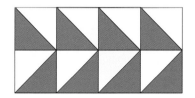

HOLY TOLEDO BORDER UNIT
Make 36 in assorted light/dark
color combinations

G

CORNER PINWHEEL UNIT
4 1/2" unfinished.
Make 4

H

HALF PINWHEEL
Make 2 each to match
each Pinwheel Corner
unit for a total of 8

ASSEMBLY DIAGRAM

Criss Cross
Applesauce

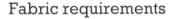

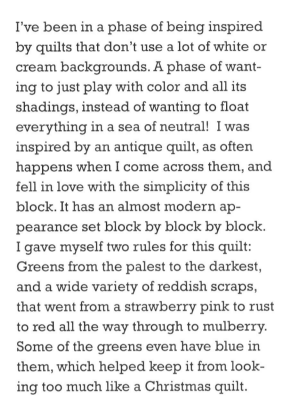

I've been in a phase of being inspired by quilts that don't use a lot of white or cream backgrounds. A phase of wanting to just play with color and all its shadings, instead of wanting to float everything in a sea of neutral! I was inspired by an antique quilt, as often happens when I come across them, and fell in love with the simplicity of this block. It has an almost modern appearance set block by block by block. I gave myself two rules for this quilt: Greens from the palest to the darkest, and a wide variety of reddish scraps, that went from a strawberry pink to rust to red all the way through to mulberry. Some of the greens even have blue in them, which helped keep it from looking too much like a Christmas quilt.

During the making of this quilt, I lost my grandfather, who lived a long, full life. I was able to incorporate a couple of his shirts in this quilt which adds so much meaning to me. The binding took every inch of one of those shirts, so now I know just how far one shirt can go!

FINISHED BLOCK SIZE: APPROXIMATELY 6 3/8"
FINISHED QUILT SIZE:
APPROXIMATELY 87" x 93"
PIECING DIAGRAMS ARE FOUND ON PAGE 44.

Fabric requirements

7 3/4 yards assorted green scraps

2 yards assorted red scraps

Criss Cross blocks

Make 156 – approximately 6 7/8" unfinished, finishing at 6 3/8".

To make 1 block:
From the green, cut:
2 – 2" x 5" rectangles

2 – 5" squares. Cut each from corner to corner on the diagonal to yield 4 corner triangles.

From the red, cut:
2 – 2" x 5" rectangles

Diagrams are on pages 44-45

A Sew 2 red rectangles on either side of 1 green rectangle. Press seams to the green rectangle.

Sub-cut into 2 – 2" x 5" units. The extra inch is for squaring up.

B Add a pieced unit on either side of 1 green rectangle. Press seams to the green center strip.

C Add 4 green triangles to all four corners. Press seams to the corners. They will be large, leaving a bit more than 1/4" seam allowance around the outside edge. Use a ruler with a 1/4" marked line to square the block down to size. Make 156.

Note: The block WILL be an odd measurement, approximately 6 7/8" unfinished. However, if your blocks are a different size, don't fret. Because this quilt is set block to block to block, as long as your blocks are the same size as each other, you will be fine!

Quilt top center

Referring to the center of the Quilt Assembly Diagram on page 45, lay out blocks 12 across and 13 down. Stitch into rows, pinning to match seams, paying attention to where the red squares from one block meet up with the red squares from the next. Join rows to complete quilt center. Press.

Borders

The red inner border is sewn to the green outer border before attaching it to the quilt. The corner blocks are added to each end of the top and bottom borders to complete the crossed corners.

Corner blocks

From the green, cut:
4 – 5" green squares

From the red, cut:
4 – 2" x 5" red rectangles
4 – 2" x 6 1/2" red rectangles

D Add 1 short red rectangle to the side of 1 green corner block. Press to the red. Add the remaining long rectangle to the bottom of the square, so the red makes an L around one corner. Press to the red. Make 4.

From the red, cut random lengths of 2" strips. Sew together on the diagonal to create a length of approximately 380". Press seams open.

From the green, cut random lengths of 5" strips. Sew together on the straight-of-grain to create a length of approximately 380". Press seams open.

Stitch the red narrow inner border to the green outer border in one long length. Press.

Lay the quilt center out on the floor, smoothing it gently. Do not tug or pull. Measure the quilt through the center from top to bottom. Cut two side borders this length.

Repeat for top and bottom borders, measuring across the quilt center, including the borders just added in the measurement. Cut top and bottom inner borders this length. Add corner blocks to either end of both top and bottom borders, rotating them as shown in quilt diagram.

Sew the side borders to the quilt sides with right sides together, pinning to match centers and ends. Ease where necessary to fit. Press seams to the borders.

Stitch the top and bottom borders to quilt center, pinning to match centers and ends, easing where necessary. Press seams to the borders.

Finishing

Criss Cross Applesauce was quilted with a sand colored thread, in a curvy pattern called Holly's Hearts, by Urban Elementz. Turn to the resources page for contact information.

Binding

I bound the quilt in the deep eggplant plaid of one of my grandpa's precious shirts. I miss you Grandpa! You will always be my Superman!

Criss Cross
Applesauce

Directions At-A-Glance

A
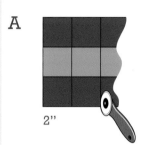
2"

B

C

CRISS CROSS BLOCK
Approximately
6 7/8" unfinished
Make 156

D

**BORDER CORNER
BLOCK**
6 1/2" unfinished
Make 4

ASSEMBLY DIAGRAM

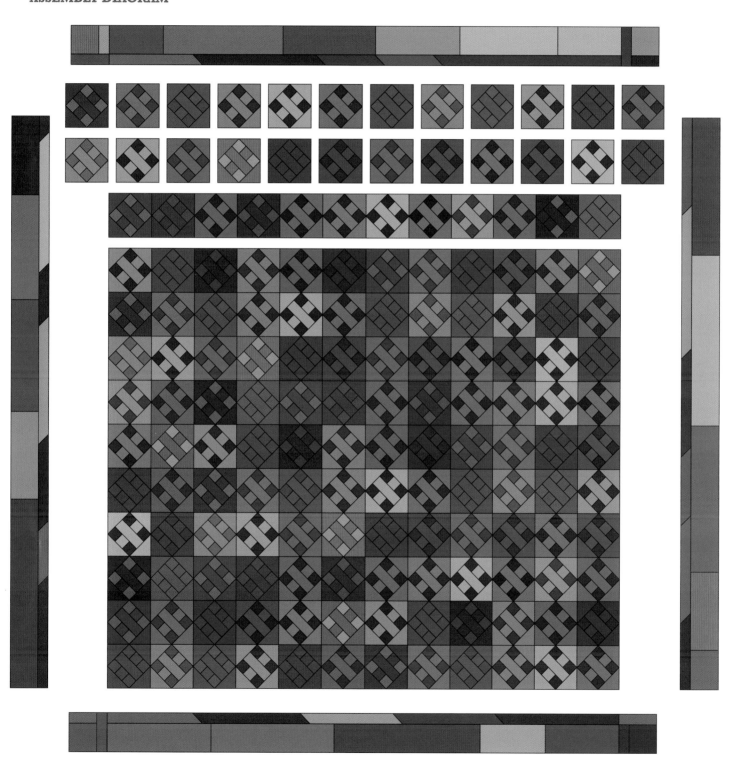

46

Hawk's Nest

I absolutely love traditional blocks and all of their interesting names and history. This block has been called such various things as Single Wedding Ring, Crown of Thorns, Nest and Fledgling, Mill Wheel, Georgetown Circle, Memory Wreath and Rolling Stone.

I started piecing these blocks on a trip to Oregon in 2009, using leftover bonus triangles saved from snowball blocks for all the half-square triangles in the quilt and the border. Playing with the coloring a little bit, I inserted the solid cheddar in the block as a way to add some punch and pizzazz to the design.

If you've been saving leftover half-square triangles from various quilting projects, this quilt is the perfect project for them. Square them down to 2" and piece away! For me, this kind of "square-down" event usually involves a TV tray, a new rotary cutter blade and a good chick-flick movie! Before you know it, your task will be done and those leftover triangles will be re-purposed into a quilt you will love!

FINISHED BLOCK SIZE: 7 1/2"

FINISHED QUILT SIZE:
APPROXIMATELY 73" x 84"

PIECING DIRECTIONS ARE FOUND ON PAGE 50.

Fabric requirements

4 1/2 yards assorted dark scraps

3 1/2 yards assorted light scraps

2 1/2 yards solid cheddar

1/2 yard red print

Hawk's Nest blocks

Make 42 – 8" unfinished, finishing at 7 1/2"

Each Hawk's Nest block is made of 16 half-square triangle units and 9 squares.

Half-square triangle units

I used my easy angle ruler and 2" strips to make the half square triangles for this block. The traditional method of using 2 3/8" squares is given for those who do not have access to this ruler. Please view section on specialty rulers for more info on using this method. You can use any method that gives you a 2" unfinished triangle unit that will finish in the quilt at 1 1/2".

To make 1 block

For the "Nest"

From the dark scraps, cut:
1 – 2" x 9" rectangle AND 2 – 2 3/8" squares from the same dark fabric.

1 – 2" square that contrasts with the dark fabric above for the block center.

From the solid cheddar, cut:
1 – 2" x 9" rectangle

2 – 2 3/8" squares

For the "Hawks"

From the dark scraps, cut: 6 – 2 3/8" squares
From the light scraps, cut: 6 – 2 3/8" squares

Note: The half-square triangles are completely scrappy within each block. If you don't want repeats, use 12 dark squares and 12 light squares, which will give you enough for two blocks. If you want to do all the triangle units ahead of time, you will need 504 half square triangles for all the blocks in this quilt. (This doesn't include the half-square triangles for the border.)

Diagrams are on page 50

A Sew the dark "Nest" rectangle and cheddar rectangle with right sides together. Press seam away from the cheddar. Sub-cut into 4 – 2" sections. There is 1" extra for trimming.

B Place 2 3/8" cheddar and 2 3/8" "Nest" squares with right sides together into matched pairs. Cut from corner to corner on the diagonal to yield 4 half square triangle pairs. Press seam away from the cheddar. Trim dog ears. Make 4. Units measure 2" unfinished, finishing at 1 1/2".

C Sew the "Hawk" half-square triangle units by placing the 6 light squares and 6 dark squares with right sides together into matched pairs. Cut from corner to corner on the diagonal to yield 12 half square triangle pairs. Stitch with a 1/4" seam allowance and press to the dark fabric. Trim dog ears. Make 12. Units measure 2" unfinished, finishing at 1 1/2".

D Arrange 3 "Hawk" triangles and one "Nest" triangle into a four-patch as shown. Stitch. Press. Make 4.

E Lay out block units with "Hawks" pointing toward corners, separated by the cheddar units. Place one random 2" scrap square as the center. Assemble the block by stitching the units into rows and joining the rows to complete the block. Make 42.

Hour-Glass blocks, half hour-glass triangles and corner triangles

Make 30 Hour-glass blocks – 8" unfinished, finishing at 7 1/2" Each Hour-Glass block is made of 2 different lights and two different darks.

Make 22 Half hour-glass triangles

Make 4 corner triangles

From the light, cut 21 – 8 3/4" squares. Cut each corner to corner with an X to yield 84 triangles.

From the dark, cut 21 – 8 3/4" squares. Cut each corner to corner with an X to yield 84 triangles.

F Arrange 120 triangles as shown and stitch 30 Hour-Glass Alternate Blocks. Press. Make 30. Units are 8" unfinished, finishing at 7 1/2".

G Arrange 44 triangles and stitch 22 half hour-glass blocks. Stitch 11 triangles with the dark on the right side and 11 with the dark on the left. Press seams to the dark fabric.

The 4 remaining triangles are the 4 corner triangles.

Quilt top center assembly

This quilt is set on point even though it doesn't look like it. This allowed me to piece the hourglass blocks with the straight of grain on the long sides of the quarter square triangles, which I found pleasing when working with plaids and stripes.

Lay out Hawk's Nest blocks on the diagonal with 6 blocks across and 7 down. Fill in the alternate block areas with the hour glass blocks, rotating the lights and darks as shown in quilt diagram. In my quilt, there is one hour glass block unit that I left turned "wrong" just for fun. See if you can find it!

Fill in the edges of the quilt with the pieced setting triangles and the corner triangles to complete the center design. Stitch quilt into diagonal rows. Join rows together to complete quilt center. Press.

Note: The corner squares will have bias on their outside edges, press these with caution, they will be stabilized when inner border is added.

Borders
Inner border

From the red print, cut: 8 – 1 3/4" strips x the width of the fabric.

Join the 8 inner border strips end to end with diagonal seams making one long length, measuring approximately 320" long. Press the seams open.

Lay quilt out on the floor, smoothing it gently. Do not tug or pull. Measure the quilt through the center from top to bottom. Cut two inner side borders this length. Sew inner side borders to the quilt sides with right sides together, pinning to match centers and ends. Ease where necessary to fit. Press seams to the borders.

Repeat for top and bottom inner borders, measuring across the quilt center, including the borders just added in the measurement. Cut top and bottom inner borders this length. Stitch top and bottom inner borders to quilt center, pinning to match centers and ends, easing where necessary. Press seams to the borders.

The "Extreme" pieced border

Are you ready? The border requires 438 half-square triangle units that finish the same 1 1/2" as the triangles in the Hawk's Nest blocks! Remember, you don't have to make them all at once, just work for an hour at a time and make more when you need more!

Half-square triangle units

From the light scraps, cut 219 – 2 3/8" squares.
From the dark scraps, cut 219 – 2 3/8" squares.

Match the squares with right sides together and slice on the diagonal from corner to corner to yield 438 triangle pairs. Stitch. Press. Trim dog ears. Units measure 2" unfinished, finishing at 1 1/2".

Border setting triangles

From the cheddar, cut:
71 – 3 3/8" squares. Cut each twice on the diagonal with an X to yield 284 triangles.

These quarter-square triangles have the straight of grain on the long edge of the triangle. This helps keep the border from stretching and flaring.

H Join 3 half-square triangle units with darks placed in position shown. Add 1 quarter square cheddar triangle to each end to form one border unit. Press.

I For the side borders, join 33 units side by side as shown in the diagram. Press. For the top and bottom borders, join 28 units side by side as shown in the diagram. Press.

Left border ends

J Piece 4 border corners as shown from 6 half-square triangle units and 4 cheddar quarter-square triangles. Add to the LEFT end of each side, top and bottom borders. Borders will not be square, but trapezoidal.

Corner units

K Arrange the triangles as shown, following the placement of the dark triangles (Please note that these are opposite of the border end triangle units!) Stitch and press. Make 8.

Join two of these end triangles to create one corner unit. Make 4.

Stitch the long edges of borders to quilt center, pinning to match ends and centers. Press. Make 4 large corner triangles. Attach large triangle corner units to quilt to complete borders. Press.

Finishing

Hawk's Nest is quilted with tan thread in an edge to edge design called Dusty Miller by Urban Elementz. See resources page for contact information.

The quilt is finished with a brown/tan stripe for old fashioned appeal. After applying binding, I noticed that some of the triangle tips were nipped off in the binding seam, but I liked the comfortable appearance it gave the quilt. My bindings are made from 2 1/2" strips and finish about 3/8" wide, just a smidge more than the traditional 1/4" seam that would have left the corners intact. If you want your triangle points, go with a binding that finishes at 1/4".

Hawks Nest

Directions At-A-Glance

A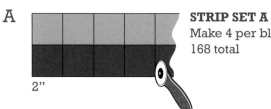

2"

STRIP SET A
Make 4 per block,
168 total

B **"NEST" HALF-SQUARE TRIANGLE UNIT**
2" unfinished
Make 4 per block,
168 total

C **"HAWK" HALF-SQUARE TRIANGLE UNIT**
2" unfinished
Make 12 per block,
504 total

D 3 1/2" unfinished
Make 4 per block,
168 total

E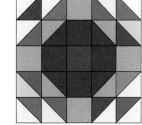

HAWK'S NEST BLOCK
8" unfinished
Make 42

F **HOUR GLASS BLOCK**
8" unfinished
Make 30

G **SETTING TRIANGLES**
Make 11 of each

BORDER

H

I

J 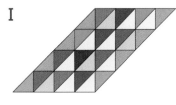 **LEFT BORDER ENDS**
Make 4

K  **CORNER UNITS**
Make 4

ASSEMBLY DIAGRAM

Stars Over Shallotte

On the eastern coast of North Carolina, about midway between Wilmington and Myrtle Beach lies the sleepy little town of Shallotte. Shallotte is the meeting place for the Brunswick Quilters Guild. While on a teaching trip there, I found myself piecing and completing this top in my hotel room during my stay.

The blocks are a traditional Double T variation, and I used leftover bonus triangles from other projects as the scrappy element in each block. The zigzag setting with four half blocks – two at the top and two at the bottom – gives this quilt an old-time, Southern feel. The blue indigo setting fabric with its white graphic design was the perfect go-along to make these stars sing.

FINISHED BLOCK SIZE: 9"

FINISHED QUILT SIZE: 82" x 94"

PIECING DIAGRAMS ARE FOUND ON PAGE 57.

Fabric requirements

For the blocks and rick rack border
3 yards assorted dark scraps

3 yards light scraps

For the setting triangles
3 yards blue

For the borders
3/4 yard red print for inner border

1 1/2 yards assorted blue scraps at least 5" wide for outer border

Double T Variation blocks

Make 28 – 9 1/2" unfinished, finishing at 9"

Each Double T Variation block is made of 4 large half-square triangle units, 16 small half-square triangle units and 1 center square.

Large half-square triangle units

Make 4 per block – 3 1/2" unfinished, finishing at 3"

I used my Easy Angle ruler and 3 1/2" strips to make the large half square triangles for this block. The traditional method of using 3 7/8" squares is given for those who do not have access to this ruler. Please view section on specialty rulers for more info on using this method. You can use any method that gives you a 3" finished half square triangle unit.

Diagrams are on pages 57 and 59

From the dark scraps, cut 2 – 3 7/8" squares. Both fabrics for each should be the same.

From the light scraps, cut 2 – 3 7/8" squares. Both fabrics for each should be the same.

A Layer the 2 large light and 2 large dark squares with right-sides together. Cut from corner to corner once on the diagonal to yield 4 matched pairs. Stitch into 4 half-square triangle units. Press to the dark and trim the dog ears.

Small half-square triangle units

Make 16 per block – 2" unfinished, finishing at 1 1/2"

I used my easy angle ruler and 2" strips to make the small half square triangles for this block. The traditional method of using 2 3/8" squares is given for those who do not have access to this ruler. Please view section on specialty rulers for more info on using this method. You can use any method that gives you a 2" unfinished half square triangle unit that finishes at 1 1/2".

From the dark scraps, cut 8 – 2 3/8" squares.

From the light scraps, cut 8 – 2 3/8" squares.

B If you do not want any small triangles to repeat within a block, use 16 different darks and 16 different lights, and you will have enough for two blocks with no repeats within the block.

Layer the 8 small dark and 8 small light squares with right-sides together. Cut from corner to corner once on the diagonal to yield 16 matched pairs. Stitch into 16 half-square triangle units. Press to the dark and trim the dog ears.

C Join the small triangle units into pairs. You will need 8 pairs of "goose units" for each block.

D Stitch two "goose units" together to make goose unit pairs. Press. Make 4.

Center block squares

Cut 1 per block – 3 1/2" unfinished

The center square can either match the large dark triangles or contrast.

From the dark or light scraps, cut 1 – 3 1/2" square.

E Lay out the block units as shown and stitch into rows. Join rows to complete each block. Press. Make 28.

Double T half block

Make 4

Each Double T half block is made of 3 large half-square triangle units, 8 small half-square triangle units and 1 center square.

Large half-square triangle units

Make 3 per block – 3 1/2" unfinished, finishing at 3"

From the dark scraps, cut 2 – 3 7/8" squares. Both fabrics for each should be the same.

From the light scraps, cut 2 – 3 7/8" squares. Both fabrics for each should be the same.

A Layer the 2 large light and 2 large dark squares with right-sides together. Cut from corner to corner once on the diagonal to yield 4 matched pairs. Stitch into 4 half-square triangle units. Press to the dark and trim the dog ears. You will only use 3 per half block. Reserve the leftover for another project.

Small half-square triangle units

Make 8 – 2" unfinished, finishing at 1 1/2"

From the dark scraps, cut 4 – 2 3/8" squares.

From the light scraps, cut 4 – 2 3/8" squares.

If you do not want any small triangles to repeat within a block, use 8 different darks and 8 different lights, and you will have enough for two blocks with no repeats within the block.

B Layer the 4 light and 4 dark squares with right-sides together. Cut from corner to corner once on the diagonal to yield 8 matched pairs. Stitch into 8 half-square triangle units. Press to the red and trim the dog ears.

Center square

Cut 1 – 3 1/2" square for the block center. This can either match the large dark triangles or contrast.

F-G Along with the center square, sew the half block together as shown in the diagram. Trim the half block 1/4" from the diagonal line, to allow for the seam allowance. Make 4.

Setting triangles

The cutting directions for the setting triangles are based on fabric that is 40" wide. If your fabric is 42" or wider, you can get by with less. Measure your fabric width and plan accordingly.

From the blue fabric, cut:

14 – 14" squares for the side setting triangles. Cut each square from corner to corner with an X to yield 56 quarter square triangles. This layout needs 54 triangles, reserve 2 for another project.

6 – 7 1/4" squares for the end triangles. Cut each square from corner to corner once on the diagonal to yield 12 end triangles

Quilt Top Center Assembly

Column A

Make 3

Column A is made of 6 full blocks on point, 10 side triangles and 4 end triangles. Referring to the Quilt Assembly Diagram, assemble the 3 columns by stitching the units into diagonal rows and joining the rows to complete the column.

Column B

Make 2

Column B is made of 5 full blocks on point with a half block on each end and 12 side triangles. Referring to the Quilt Assembly Diagram, assemble the 2 columns by stitching the units into diagonal rows and joining the rows to complete the column.

Join the 5 columns starting with Column A to complete the quilt top center.

Borders

Inner border

Turning blocks on point can mean taking a nice even block measurement and turning it into something strange! I used the inner border as a spacer between the pieced border and the quilt center to build the center up to a measurement that will fit the pieced border. Sometimes this means that your top and bottom inner border might be a slightly different width than the side inner borders if you are going by "correct" math. However, pieced borders are stretchy, and it is easy to take in a bit or let out a bit here and there in between the pieced outer border units to get the pieced border to fit the quilt the way I want.

From red print, cut 8 – 1 3/4" strips x the width of the fabric.

Join the 8 inner border strips end to end with diagonal seams to make a strip approximately 320" long. Press seams open.

Lay the quilt center out on the floor, smoothing it gently. Do not tug or pull. Measure the quilt through the center from top to bottom. Cut two inner side borders this length. Sew the inner side borders to the quilt sides with right sides together, pinning to match centers and ends. Ease where necessary to fit. Press seams to the borders.

Repeat for top and bottom inner borders, measuring across the quilt center, including the borders just added in the measurement. Cut top and bottom inner borders this length. Stitch the top and bottom inner borders to quilt center, pinning to match centers and ends, easing where necessary. Press seams to borders.

Rick rack border

I love wonky quilts, so an uneven rick-rack-type border was perfect to frame the quilt center!

From the light scraps, cut:

100 – 3 1/2" squares.

From the dark scraps, cut:

100 – 2" squares. Draw a line from corner to corner on the back of the squares.

100 – 2 1/2" squares. Draw a line from corner to corner on the back of the squares.

Bonus triangles

H-J When the corner squares are at least 2 1/2" wide, this is an opportunity for me to do a bit of extra sewing to give me bonus half-square triangle units, rather than just a handful of trimmed off "waste" triangles. I mark a scant 3/8" line from the center diagonal line on the 2 1/2" dark squares only (The 2" ones are too small to deal with – those go into crumb piecing!) and sew both seams. This is an optional step of course, but I like having bonus units around that I can quickly use as "Quilt Seeds" to work into a new design later. This is how I ended up with so many scrappy triangles in the blocks of this quilt in the first place!

Lay 1 – 2 1/2" dark marked square in one corner of 1 – 3 1/2" light square with your second bonus line placed toward the corner as shown. Stitch on the first diagonal line, and finger press to make sure the dark square folds over to meet the edges of the base unit properly. If it does, stitch on the second line.

Note: depending on the thickness of your thread, and your fabric, it may give you better results to stitch just to the "inside of the channel" between the two lines. Make a test block and measure to see if your pieces are coming out the right size.

Trim between the two lines and press. Test your bonus triangle. It should measure 2". If it is a bit too small, you will need to skinny down your seam allowance by stitching a bit closer to the diagonal line. Test to find out what you need to do to adjust your seams resulting in bonus units that are a useable size. 2" is great – 1 7/8" will give you squares that are harder to use.

Hint: In my classes I have also told students to take a 2" square of template plastic, slice it on the diagonal, (One for you, one for a friend!) and use that as the guide for drawing the second line by placing it in the corner of the square. One line on the diagonal and a drawn line using the 2" triangle give good results!

Add the smaller corner triangles in the same manner, placing them in the opposite diagonal corner of the base block and sewing from corner to corner. Finger press to be sure the square folds back to meet the edges of the base unit. Trim the excess. Make 100.

K Match the large corner triangles together in pairs and stitch. Make 48 pairs.

Stars Over Shallotte

Directions At-A-Glance

A

LARGE HALF-SQUARE TRIANGLE UNIT
3 1/2" unfinished
Make 4 per block, 464 total

B

SMALL HALF-SQUARE TRIANGLE UNIT
2" unfinished
Make 16 per block and 8 per half block, 464 total

C

GOOSE UNIT
3 1/2" x 2" unfinished
Make 8 pairs per block and 4 per half block, 232 total

D
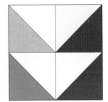

GOOSE UNIT PAIRS
3 1/2" square unfinished
Make 4 per block and 2 per half block, 116 total

E
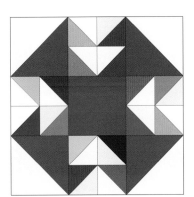

DOUBLE T VARIATION BLOCK
9 1/2" unfinished
Make 28

F
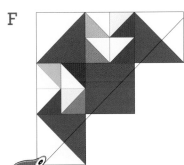

G

HALF DOUBLE T BLOCK
Make 4

H

I

J

BORDER UNIT
2" unfinished
Make 100

K

BORDER UNIT
3 1/2" x 2" unfinished
Make 48 pairs

Side rick rack borders

Join 13 pairs end-to-end for each side border. If the border is too long for the quilt, now is the time to take the border up a bit in between the seams to get it to fit. If it is too tight for the quilt, you can simply let out some seams, sewing a scant seam allowance to make the border fit. Add to the quilt with large triangles up against inner border, pinning to match ends and centers. Stitch. Press seams toward inner border.

Top and bottom rick rack borders

Join 11 border unit pairs end to end for each top and bottom border. Add an extra single unit to each end of both top and bottom borders as corner units. Adjust between seams to get border to fit if needed. Pin to match centers and ends and stitch to quilt. Press seams toward inner border.

Outer blue border

From the assorted blue scraps, cut random lengths into 5" wide strips. Join the strips end-to-end on the straight of grain to create a length of approximately 320". Press.

Lay quilt out on the floor, smoothing it gently. Do not tug or pull. Measure the quilt through the center from top to bottom. Cut two outer side borders this length. Sew borders to the quilt sides with right sides together, pinning to match centers and ends. Ease where necessary to fit. Press seams to the borders.

Repeat for top and bottom blue borders, measuring across the quilt center, including the borders just added in the measurement. Cut top and bottom borders this length. Stitch top and bottom borders to quilt center, pinning to match centers and ends, easing where necessary. Press seam to borders.

Finishing

Stars over Shallotte is quilted with blue thread in an edge-to-edge design called Tail Feathers designed by Hermoine Agee of Lorien Quilting. Turn to the resources page for contact information.

The quilt is bound in a rust colored paisley to finish, bringing the color of the inner border to the edge of the quilt.

ASSEMBLY DIAGRAM

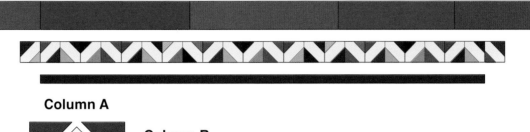

Column A

Column B

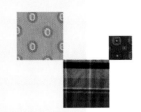

Old Kentucky Album

Blue plaids from recycled shirts and double pink scraps from my 2" strip bin were the beginnings of this project. One blue and one pink for each block seemed pretty simple, but what if a strip was too short to get all 4 pink rectangles needed? Just as in times past, I simply substituted another pink, mixing and un-matching them as I went! Pretty soon I was even daring to boldly use those old mauve and dusty rose calicoes that were so popular in the 1980s and 1990s. They worked just fine, proving that fabric does NOT have an expiration date! The backgrounds vary in shade from light white all the way through to a golden tan, giving the quilt an aged appearance as well.

FINISHED BLOCK SIZE: 8 1/4"

FINISHED QUILT SIZE: 86 1/2" x 97 3/4"

PIECING DIAGRAMS ARE FOUND ON PAGE 64-65.

Fabric requirements

For the blocks

1 1/2 yards assorted blue scraps

1 yard assorted scraps in a variety of colors from pink to raspberry.

2 1/2 yards light/neutral scraps

For the sashing, borders and cornerstones

3 1/2 yards brown print

2 yards double pink print

1 3/4 yards blue print

Old Kentucky Album block

Make 42 – 8 3/4" unfinished, finishing at 8 1/4"

The Old Kentucky block is made of strips and squares to avoid piecing the outer triangles and is squared to size after piecing.

To make 1 block

From the light/neutral, cut:
2 – 2" x 13" rectangles

8 – 2" squares

From the blue, cut:
1 – 2" x 13" rectangle

1 – 2" x 5" rectangle

From the pink, cut:
4 – 2" x 5" rectangles

Block center unit
Diagrams are on pages 64-65

A Sew 2 long, light rectangles to either side of 1 long, blue rectangle. Press to the blue. Sub-cut into 6 – 2" segments. There is an extra inch in the length of the strip set for trimming and squaring. Note: 2 will be used for the center unit and 4 will be used for the corner units.

B Sew 2 pieced units to either side of 1 short, blue rectangle. Press to the blue.

C Add 2 pink rectangles to either side of the center unit. Press seams to the pink.

D Stitch 2 light squares to either side of the remaining 2 pink rectangles. Press seams to the pink and add these units to the top and bottom of the block center. Press to the units just added.

Block corner units

E Center a square to 1 leftover pieced light/blue/light unit made above. The edges of the light square will extend 1/4" beyond the seams of the blue square. Make 4.

Add the 4 block corner units to the center unit, centering them over the pink rectangles. The corner units will extend beyond the pink 1/4" on either side. Press to the pink.

Hint: I find it helpful to use a bit of spray sizing or starch when I press, to help stabilize the block before trimming. A bit of stiffness also helps keep bias edges from stretching.

F-G Trim the block 1/4" away from all colored points to square up the block. The block will measure approximately 8 3/4" at this point. If your block measures differently, don't fret. What is important is that your blocks all measure the same as each other. Make 42.

Quilt top assembly

Sashing

From the brown, cut 97 – 3 1/2" x 8 3/4" rectangles.

Note: If your block is a different measurement, cut the rectangles the same length as your block size.

Cornerstones

From the pink, cut 56 – 3 1/2" squares.

Referring to the Quilt Assembly Diagram on page 65, lay out the blocks in rows along with the sashing pieces and the pink cornerstones. Stitch the quilt center into rows, pressing seams toward the sashing, and away from the cornerstones. Join the rows to complete quilt center.

Borders

Though this quilt looks like it has multiple borders, The 5 different borders are sewn together in one long panel, and the border lengths are then cut from the panel. The stars are added as cornerstones.

From blue fabric, cut 20 – 2 1/2" strips x the width of fabric.

From pink fabric, cut 20 – 1 1/2" strips x the width of fabric.

From brown fabric, cut 10 – 2 1/2" strips x the width of fabric

Join each fabric end to end with diagonal seams in lengths of 10 strips each. Trim excess and press the seams open. You will have 5 long lengths, each approximately 400" long.

Sew the pink borders to either side of the brown center border. Press seams to the pink border. Sew the blue borders to either side of the pink borders. Press seams to the pink borders.

Lay quilt out on the floor, smoothing it gently. Do not tug or pull. Measure the quilt through the center from top to bottom. Cut two side borders this length.

Repeat for top and bottom borders, measuring across the quilt center, from side to side. Cut the top and bottom borders this length.

Corner stars

From the same blue used in the border, cut:
16 - 2 1/2" squares

From a different blue, cut:
4 – 3 3/8" squares

From the same brown as used in the border, cut: 8 – 2 7/8" squares. Cut each on the diagonal from corner to corner to yield 16 triangles.

From light/neutral, cut:

16 – 2 7/8" squares. Cut each on the diagonal from corner to corner to yield 32 triangles.

From pink, cut:

4 – 5 1/4" squares. Cut each corner to corner twice with an X to yield 16 quarter square triangles.

H Stitch a light triangle to either side of each pink triangle. Press seams to the light triangles. Trim dog ears Make 4 for each star, 16 total.

I Stitch 4 brown triangles to blue 3 3/8" squares, pressing seams toward the brown triangles. Trim dog ears. Make 4.

J Lay out the pieces as shown in the diagram, and stitch block units into rows, joining rows to complete each block. Press

Sew side borders to the quilt center with right sides together, pinning to match centers and ends. Ease where necessary to fit. Press seams to the borders.

Sew a corner star to each end of both top and bottom borders. Press to the border. Add the top and bottom borders to the quilt with right sides together, pinning to match centers and ends. Ease where necessary to fit. Press seams to the borders.

Finishing

Old Kentucky Album is quilted edge to edge in traditional Baptist fans using a light blue thread. I would have to say that if I could, I would put Baptist fans on EVERYTHING, there is just not a quilt around that doesn't look great with fans!

The quilt is bound with the remaining brown fabric used for the quilt sashing and borders.

Old Kentucky Album

Directions At-A-Glance

A
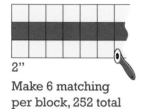
2"
Make 6 matching
per block, 252 total

B

C
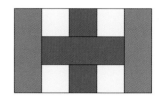

D
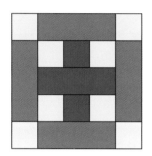

E

F
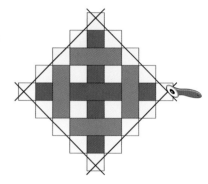

G

**OLD KENTUCKY
ALBUM**
8 3/4" unfinished
Make 42

BORDER

H

2 1/2" x 4 1/2" unfinished
Make 4 each in matching
colors, 16 total

I
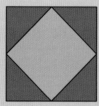
4 1/2" unfinished
Make 4

J
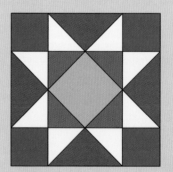

CORNER STAR
8 1/2" unfinished
Make 4

64

ASSEMBLY DIAGRAM

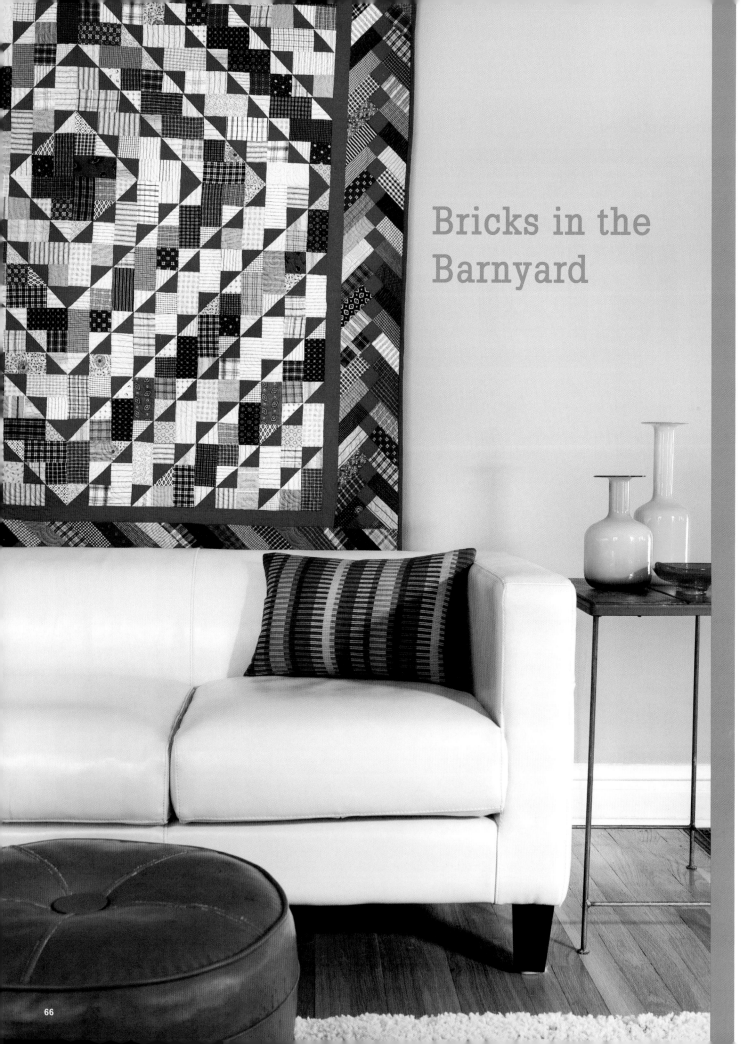

Bricks in the Barnyard

Simple shapes such as bricks, squares and triangles combine in a dynamic design perfect for using up the leftovers from other recycled projects! I find myself time and time again gravitating toward bold colors to mix with my recycled fabrics in the time honored tradition of mixing solids, prints, stripes and plaids together. Solid fabrics pack a lot of punch! In this case, the red just glows with warmth against the myriad of other cherished recycled pieces.

Pieced braids are a fun way to frame a quilt, and I love how the scraps seem to flow in motion around the outside edge like arrows. No mitering, no centering, the braids are built simply until they are "long enough" and cut where needed to fit. It's a perfect relaxed solution with no stress required!

FINISHED BLOCK SIZE: 6"

FINISHED QUILT SIZE: APPROXIMATELY 62 1/2" x 75 1/2"

PIECING DIAGRAMS ARE FOUND ON PAGE 70-71.

Fabric requirements

For blocks and outer border
3 1/2 yards assorted dark fabrics

2 1/2 yards assorted light fabrics

For accent and inner border
2 1/2 yards solid red

Split Bricks blocks

Make 80 – Blocks measure 6 1/2" unfinished, finishing at 6".

Each block requires 3 half-square triangle units, 2 bricks and 2 squares.

Half-square triangle units

I used my Easy Angle ruler and 2 1/2" strips to make the half square triangles for this block. The traditional method of using 2 7/8" squares is given for those who do not have access to this ruler. Please view section on specialty rulers for more info on using this method. You can use any method that gives you a 2" finished half square triangle unit.

From the light scraps, cut 120 – 2 7/8" squares.

From the solid red, cut 120 – 2 7/8" squares.

Diagrams are on pages 70-71

A Lay the light squares with red squares right sides together and slice on the diagonal from corner to corner yielding 240 half-square triangle pairs. Stitch. Press to the red. Units measure 2 1/2" unfinished, finishing at 2".

Bricks and squares

B From light scraps, cut:

80 – 2 1/2" x 4 1/2" rectangles

80 – 2 1/2" squares

C From dark scraps, cut:

80 – 2 1/2" x 4 1/2" rectangles

80 – 2 1/2" squares

D Lay out triangle units, bricks and squares as shown, placing the red triangles up against the lighter units. Stitch the block into rows, joining the rows to complete each block. Make 80.

Quilt top center assembly

Referring to the Quilt Assembly Diagram on page 71, lay out the blocks in rows of 8 blocks across, and 10 blocks down, arranging them in a "barn raising" fashion. I personally find it easiest to start at the quilt center and work out to get the pattern running the right direction.

Stitch blocks into rows, and join rows to complete quilt center. Press.

Note: Did you know that this is similar to a log cabin block? You can arrange these in many log cabin layouts. Take time to play with them while you are laying them out and you might find yourself creating your own design!

Borders
Inner border

From the red, cut 7 – 2" wide strips x the width of the fabric.

Join the strips end to end with diagonal seams to make one long length, measuring approximately 280". Press the seams open.

Lay quilt out on the floor, smoothing it gently. Do not tug or pull. Measure the quilt through the center from top to bottom. Cut two inner side borders this length. Sew inner side borders to the quilt sides with right sides together, pinning to match centers and ends. Ease where necessary to fit. Press seams to the borders.

Repeat for top and bottom inner borders, measuring across the quilt center, including the borders just added in the measurement. Stitch top and bottom inner borders to quilt center, pinning to match centers and ends, easing where necessary. Press seams to the borders.

Braid border

From the dark scraps, cut 320 – 2" x 5" rectangles.

From the red, cut 160 – 2" squares.

You will need approximately 80 rectangles for each of the 4 borders. The borders are pieced to fit the quilt, and then cut where you need them to be cut, so making this border larger for a larger quilt is easy!

Depending on the length of your quilt center, the amount of braid rectangles you need to make this border may vary. Numbers given are a good starting point.

E Step 1 Start to build your braid by stitching 1 red square to the end of 1 rectangle. Press to the rectangle. Stitch another rectangle to the left of this unit as shown, forming an L. The braid will be squared off at the end later. This is just to get your shape going!

F Step 2 Attach another dark rectangle to the unit, aligning the top of the rectangle with the top of the red square. Sew another red square to another rectangle, and add that to the growing braid.

Hint: I often find myself making 2 braids at once, using each as the "Leader & Ender" for the other one to keep the piecing continuous! This saves on lots of wasted thread mess!

G-H Step 3 Continue to add plain rectangles, and the rectangles with squares alternately to the braid. Build 2 braids about 10" longer than the sides of the quilt. You will lose some in the trimming process. Square off the bottom of the braid, and even up the edges as shown in the trimming diagram.

Lay quilt out on the floor, smoothing it gently. Do not tug or pull. Measure the quilt through the center from top to bottom. Cut two side borders this length. It does not matter if you cut through the red squares. The border ends where the border ends!

Sew side borders to the quilt sides with right sides together, pinning to match centers and ends. Ease where necessary to fit. Press seams to the inner red borders.

At this point, use the trimmed off parts from the braid TOPS as starters to continue building your two remaining braids for the top and bottom of the quilt. Follow the same method for trimming the side borders, and lay the borders across the quilt center from side to side, including the side braid borders in the measurement. Cut two borders this size. Stitch top and bottom borders to quilt center, pinning to match centers and ends, easing where necessary. Press.

Finishing

I love whirly swirly quilting textures, especially when the quilt is so busy that intricate heirloom quilting will be lost. For this quilt I chose a pattern designed by Hermione Agee of Lorien Quilting called "Check and Chase." I quilted it fairly close for lots of texture using an antique gold colored thread. Refer to the resources on page 94 for information.

A solid red binding finishes off the quilt, bringing the red from the quilt center all the way to the edge.

Bricks in the Barnyard

Directions At-A-Glance

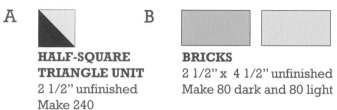

A

HALF-SQUARE TRIANGLE UNIT
2 1/2" unfinished
Make 240

B

BRICKS
2 1/2" x 4 1/2" unfinished
Make 80 dark and 80 light

C

SQUARES
2 1/2" square unfinished
Make 80 dark and
80 light

D

SPLIT BRICK BLOCK
6 1/2" unfinished
Make 80

E

Step 1

F

Step 2

G

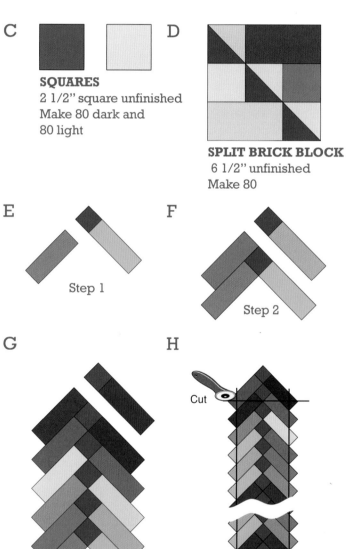

Step 3

H

Cut

Trimming Guide

ASSEMBLY DIAGRAM

Oregon or Bust!

Simple antique quilts made to keep families warm inspired this quilt. Each year I am lucky enough to spend the second week of July with a wonderful group of quilters retreating away at my friend Randy's house. We sew and sew and laugh and take walks through the beautiful surroundings, ride bikes along the river, keep our eyes open for deer and other wildlife, eat and eat and sew some more! We cap the end of our quilting week off by spending the day in Sisters, Oregon enjoying the annual quilt show. I kitted up the fabrics for this quilt, cutting my strips and squares ahead of time so they would fit in my luggage. Just like pioneers of old, I was making my way to Oregon, or Bust!

FINISHED BLOCK SIZE: 9"

FINISHED QUILT SIZE:
APPROXIMATELY 85" x 100"

PIECING DIAGRAMS ARE FOUND ON PAGE 76.

Fabric requirements

For the blocks
2 yards light/neutral shirt fabrics and shirting scraps
4 yards assorted dark scraps

For sashing and cornerstones
2 yards of deep gold/orange
1/2 yard of assorted red scraps

For the setting triangles
1 1/2 yard blue gingham

For the borders
1/2 yard black stripe
1 1/2 yards red print

Oregon or Bust block

Make 50 – 9 1/2" unfinished, finishing at 9".

This block is easily constructed with one strip set, plus 2 extra 1 1/2" squares. Four 3 1/2" corner squares complete the block.

Strip set for nine-patch and rail units

When planning strip sets, I chose two colors that worked well together. I wasn't paying attention to medium/light/dark, just the color! The light fabrics do go in the corners of the block.

From the assorted dark fabrics, cut:
2 – 1 1/2" wide x 20" strip of Color 1. Remember when working with scraps cut from recycled clothing, some strips will be shorter than others, so more strips may be needed to get the block sections required. If you cut from scraps and not width of fabric yardage, plan accordingly.

1 – 1 1/2" wide x 20" strip of Color 2.

2 – 1 1/2" squares of Color 2.

Diagrams are on page 76

A Sew the strip set with the Color 2 fabric in between the Color 1 fabrics. Press seams toward the outside strips.

From the strip set cut the following:
4 – 3 1/2" segments for the rail units.

3 – 1 1/2" segments for nine-patch center segment.

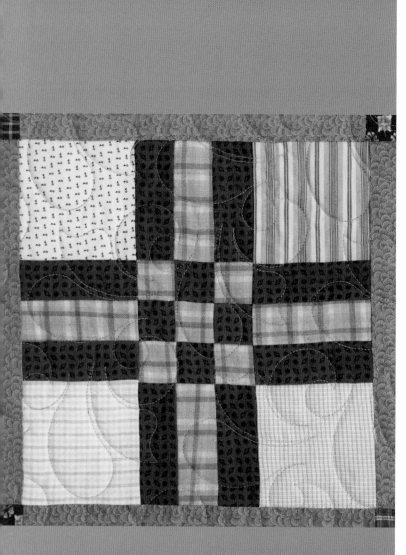

B Remove a 1 1/2" Color 1 square from TWO of the nine-patch center segments, and sew the 2 extra Color 2 squares on the opposite end of the segment.

C Make 1 nine-patch center unit using the three segments.

Corner squares

D **From the light/neutral shirt fabrics and shirting scraps, cut:**
200 – 3 1/2" squares.

Lay out the 4 rail units, 1 nine-patch unit and the 4 corner squares in a nine-patch format, and stitch. Press. Make 50.

Sashing and cornerstones

From the deep gold/orange, cut:
120 – 2" x 9 1/2" rectangles.

From the assorted reds, cut:
49 – 2" squares.

6 – 3 1/2" squares. Cut each square on the diagonal twice with an X to yield 24 half cornerstones. You will only use 22. Reserve the other two for another project.

Setting triangles

From the blue gingham, cut:
5 – 14" squares. Cut each square on the diagonal twice with an X to yield 20 large side triangles.

2 – 7 1/4" squares. Cut each square once on the diagonal to yield 4 corner triangles.

Referring to the Quilt Assembly Diagram on page 77, lay out the blocks, sashing and cornerstones, and the side and corner setting triangles.

The rows will be pieced diagonally with sashing in between the blocks. Setting triangles are added to the end of each row as they are constructed. This is followed by a sashing row made from sashing and cornerstones, ending with a half cornerstone at each end.

On the block rows, press seams away from the blocks and toward the sashing. On the sashing rows, press the seams away from the cornerstones. This will help seams to nest in quilt construction.

Piece the quilt into rows, joining the rows into two approximate quilt halves. Then join the halves together to complete the quilt center. This helps distribute some of the weight as the quilt center grows bigger with each row added.

Before the inner border is added, trim the quilt center so the corners are at proper right angles and any dog ears are trimmed, leaving 1/4" seam allowance around the outside edge of the top.

Inner border

From the black stripe, cut 9 – 1 1/2" wide strips x the width of fabric.

Join the strips end to end with diagonal seams to make a border measuring approximately 300" long. Press seams open.

Lay quilt out on the floor, smoothing it gently. Do not tug or pull. Measure the quilt through the center from top to bottom. Cut two inner side borders this length. Sew inner side borders to the quilt sides with right sides together, pinning to match centers and ends. Ease where necessary to fit. Press seams to the borders.

Repeat for top and bottom inner borders, measuring across the quilt center, including the borders just added in the measurement. Stitch top and bottom inner borders to quilt center, pinning to match centers and ends, easing where necessary. Press seams to the borders.

Outer border

From the red print, cut 9 – 5" wide x the width of fabric strips.

Join the strips end to end on the straight of grain to make a strip measuring approximately 360" long. Press the seams open. Add the outer border in the same manner as the inner borders were added. Press seams to the outer borders.

Finishing

Oregon or Bust is quilted with a sand colored thread in a lovely feathery edge to edge design called Ambrosia designed by Hermione Agee of Lorien Quilting, Australia. Turn to the resources page for contact information.

Binding

A black binding finishes it off, echoing the black inner border.

Oregon or Bust

Directions At-A-Glance

A

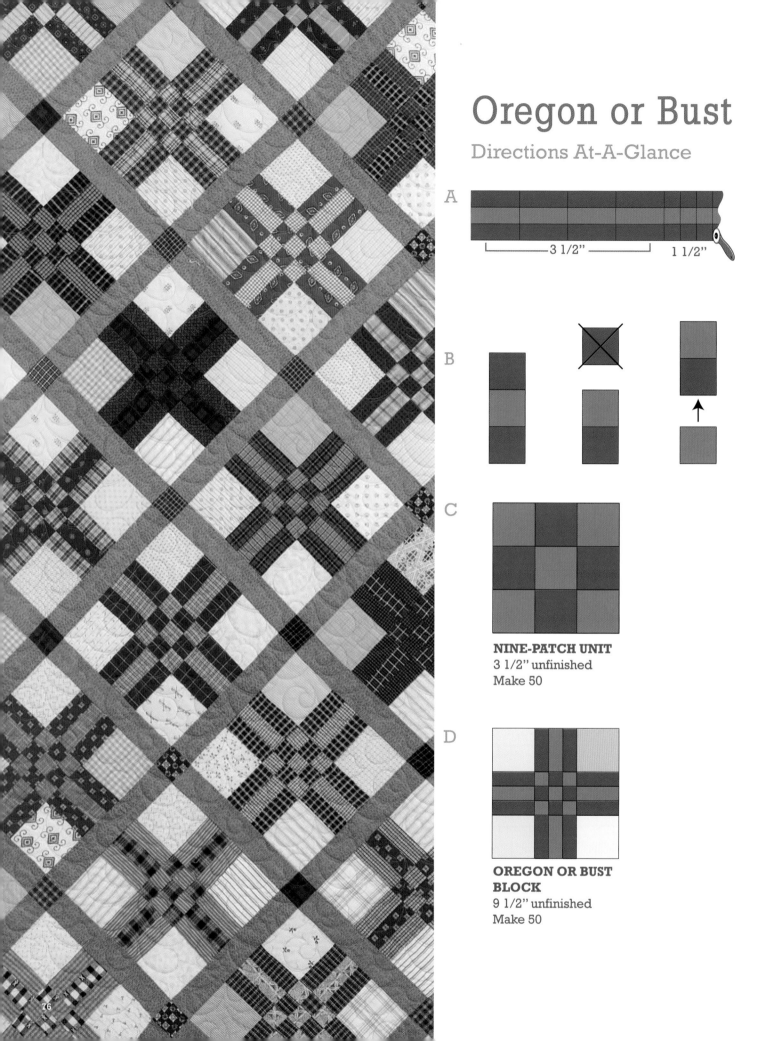

├─── 3 1/2" ───┤ 1 1/2"

B

C

NINE-PATCH UNIT
3 1/2" unfinished
Make 50

D

OREGON OR BUST BLOCK
9 1/2" unfinished
Make 50

Rectangle
Wrangle

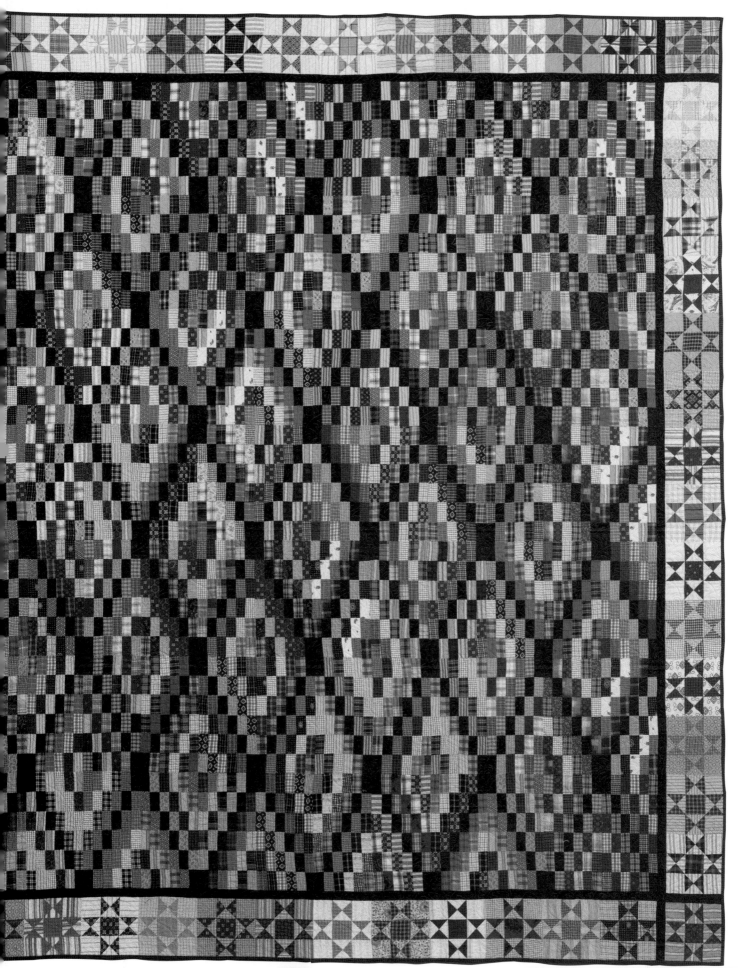

Rectangle Wrangle

Bargello style quilts have always appealed to me. Scrappy ones of course, are a favorite! This one is another take on **Bargello in Plaid** which appeared in the original **Scraps & Shirttails** book. My mind often plays with options, and this one soon followed. What would happen if I cut the constructed panels into rectangles instead of squares? Could I arrange them some way that the design would emphasize the diamond pattern I had in my head? Solid black on the diagonal was the ticket, and this is the result!

FINISHED BLOCK SIZE: 6" x 12"

FINISHED QUILT SIZE:

APPROXIMATELY 86" x 98"

PIECING DIAGRAMS ARE FOUND ON PAGE 83-84.

Fabric requirements

For the blocks and borders
2 yards black solid

10 1/2 yards assorted light and dark shirting scraps

Uphill and Downhill blocks

Make 42 Uphill blocks and 42 Downhill blocks – 6 1/2" x 12 1/2" unfinished, finishing at 6" x 12".

The panels in the quilt center are constructed from 6 – 2 1/2" strips, with the black strip either progressing uphill or downhill on the diagonal center of each block.

From the black, cut:
21 – 2 1/2" strips x the width of fabric. From each strip sub-cut 4 – 2 1/2" x 10" strips for a total of 84.

From the assorted light and dark scraps, cut:
420 – 2 1/2" x 10" strips

Diagrams are on pages 83-84

A For one panel, sew 5 scrap strips and one black strip together as shown. Press all the seams in one direction. Half of these will be reversed and repressed after cutting for ease of matching seams.

Sew the panel into a tube by bringing the bottom black strip up to match the top strip with right sides together. Carefully fold your tube so it is straight and flat. Align the edges as best as you can and trim off the edge so it is straight. An extra 1" has been added in to the strip measurement for squaring and trimming your panel.

Cut the panel tube into 6 – 1 1/2" sections.

B To make 1 UPHILL block, take 1 loop and carefully unstitch the seam between the black rectangle and the rectangle next to it, opening the loop into a row of 6 rectangles.

Hint: Seam rippers can get dull too! If your seam ripper isn't doing a good job, treat yourself to a new one. I open seams by slicing through every third or fourth stitch and then gently lifting the pieces apart from each other. Do not force a seam to open or you might rip the fabric! Because I have great experience with "un-sewing" I tend to use a stitch length long enough that I can get the point of the seam ripper under those stitches if I have to!

Take the second looped strip and open the strip so the black rectangle is one "stair step" up from the first. The black rectangles are going to go up one position from corner to corner from bottom left to upper right in the uphill block.

Finger press the seams in the opposite direction so they oppose the seams in the first strip. Sew the two sections together with a 1/4" seam allowance and finger press seam in one direction.

Note: This requires finger pressing at this stage. We will do the final pressing once we know which way the blocks will face in their final layout. This will prevent a lot of re-pressing in the construction. When the quilt is laid out and blocks are sewn together, we will press row 1 in one direction and row 2 in the opposite direction so seams will butt each other all the way across the quilt.

Add strips 3, 4, 5 and 6 in the same manner, finger pressing seams in one direction to complete one uphill block. Make 42.

C Following the same process, make 42 Downhill blocks, with the black rectangles stair stepping down from the upper left to the bottom right of the block.

Lay out blocks as shown in the Quilt Assembly Diagram on page 84, alternating Uphill blocks with Downhill blocks. There are 12 blocks across and 7 blocks down. Please note that you can rotate your block for the best color placement, but no matter which way you turn the blocks they will remain uphill or downhill only. Look at the back of the blocks too. Depending on the way you turn them, you may find that seams do not always butt. Sometimes I find myself having to twist a seam to get it to be where I want it to be. I do a lot of iron mashing at this point! It happens. Sometimes rotating the block can put it in a position where seams do butt up nicely.

Stitch the blocks into rows, pressing all the long seams in the "odd" rows in one direction, all the long seams in the "even" rows in the opposite direction. Join the rows to complete the quilt center. Press.

Ohio Star border blocks

Make 56 – 6 1/2" unfinished, finishing at 6".

Ohio Stars are the perfect frame for this quilt. I used all light scraps for the star backgrounds because I thought the center of the quilt was quite dark. This let the light in!

To make 1 block:

From the light scraps, cut:
4 – 2 1/2" squares

2 – 3 1/4" squares

From the dark scraps, cut:
1 – 2 1/2" square

2 – 3 1/4" squares

Hour-glass units

I used my Companion Angle ruler and 1 1/2" strips to make the hour-glass units for this block. The traditional method for piecing is given for those who do not have access to this ruler. Please view section on specialty rulers for more info on using this method. You can use any method that gives you a 2" finished hour-glass unit.

D Place the large dark and light squares with right sides together and cut with an X from corner to corner to yield 8 triangle pairs. Stitch the pairs together and press to create 8 half hour-glass units. Stitch units together to create 4 hour-glass units. Press and trim dog ears.

E Lay out block pieces in format shown. Stitch units into rows, and join rows to complete one star. Press. Make 56. Units are 6 1/2" unfinished, finishing at 6".

Rectangle Wrangle
Directions At-A-Glance

Border Assembly

From the black, cut 9 - 1 1/2" strips X the width of the fabric.

Join 8 of the strips with diagonal seams to form one long length measuring approximately 320". Trim excess 1/4" beyond the diagonal seams and press seams open.

From the remaining black strip, cut 4 - 1 1/2" x 6-1/2" rectangles for the top and bottom border spacers.

For the side borders, join 14 stars end to end. Press.

For top and bottom borders, join 12 stars end to end. Press.

Lay the quilt on the floor smoothing it gently. Do not tug or pull. Measure the quilt through the center from top to bottom. Cut two inner side borders this length.

Sew the inner side borders to the side star borders with right sides together, pinning to match centers and ends, easing where necessary. Press seams toward the black inner border.

Attach side borders to quilt center, pinning to match centers and ends, easing where necessary. Press seams toward the black inner border.

Measure the quilt through the center from side to side including the borders just added in the measurement. Cut two top and bottom black inner borders this length.

Attach a 1 1/2" x 6 1/2" rectangle spacer to each end of the top and bottom star borders. Press seams toward the black spacer. Stitch a corner star block to each end of the top and bottom borders on either side of the spacer. Press seam toward the black spacer.

Stitch the top and bottom inner black border to the top and bottom borders. Press seams toward the black inner border.

Attach top and bottom borders to the quilt, pinning centers and ends and easing where necessary. Press seam toward the black inner border.

Finishing

Rectangle Wrangle was quilted with an antique gold thread using a design called "Agave" by Urban Elementz. See resources page for contact information.

My original thought was to bind this quilt in black, but it was just too stark for the feel of the quilt! I compromised, using a brown/black gingham that still tied in with the black, but warmed up the appearance.

A
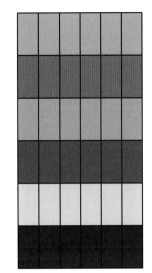
Make 84

B

UPHILL PANEL BLOCK
6 1/2" x 12 1/2" unfinished
Make 42

C

DOWNHILL PANEL BLOCK
6 1/2" x 12 1/2" unfinished
Make 42

D

QUARTER-SQUARE TRIANGLE UNIT
2 1/2" square unfinished
Make 224 in sets of 4 per color

E
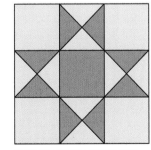
OHIO STAR BLOCK
6 1/2" unfinished
Make 56

ASSEMBLY DIAGRAM

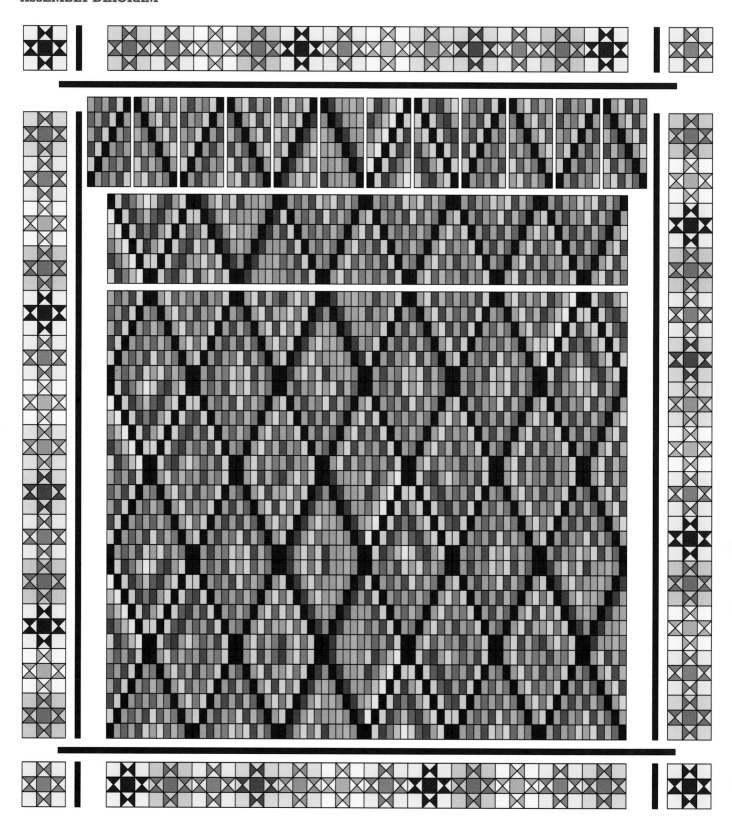

Carolina
Christmas

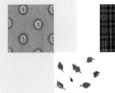

Carolina Christmas

I designed **Carolina Christmas** in a personal attempt to use up red and green recycled fabrics, blending them with Christmas fabrics and other neutral scraps. I love to put holiday quilts on the beds in my house! Nothing brightens a room and gives it new life like switching out the quilts on the bed.

This quilt was a great one for digging into my scrap bins of 2 1/2" strips – pulling out the reds, greens and neutrals. I used one common gold fabric to tie everything together, but you could go scrappy there too if you wanted!

FINISHED BLOCK SIZE: 16"

FINISHED QUILT SIZE: 92" SQUARE

PIECING DIAGRAMS ARE FOUND ON PAGES 90-92.

Fabric requirements

For blocks and outer border
6 yards of light scraps
3 1/2 yards assorted green scraps
3 yards assorted red scraps
1 1/4 yards gold print

For inner border
3/4 yard beige stripe

Carolina Star block

Make 13 – 16 1/2" unfinished, finishing at 16".

The Carolina Star block is made of 4 Fox and Geese units.

Fox units

Make 108 – 4 1/2" unfinished, finishing at 4"

From the red scraps, cut:
108 – 2 7/8" squares

From the neutral scraps, cut:
108 – 2 7/8" squares

216 – 2 1/2" squares

Half-square triangle units

I used my Easy Angle ruler and 2 1/2" strips to make the half square triangles for this block. The traditional method of using 2 7/8" squares is given for those who do not have access to this ruler. Please view section on specialty rulers for more info on using this method. You can use any method that gives you a 2" finished half square triangle unit.

Diagrams are on pages 90-92

A Match the red 2 7/8" squares to the neutral 2 7/8" squares with right sides together. Slice on the diagonal to yield 216 triangle pairs. Stitch with 1/4" seam allowance. Press. Trim dog ears. Make 216. Units measure 2 1/2" unfinished, finishing at 2".

B Arrange half square triangles with neutral 2 1/2" squares as shown. Stitch. Press. Make 108 Fox units. They measure 8 1/2" unfinished. Use 104 for the blocks and 4 for the pieced outer border.

Geese Units

Make 104 – 4 1/2" unfinished, finishing at 4"

From the green scraps, cut:
52 – 2 7/8" squares

52 – 4 7/8" squares

From the neutral scraps, cut:
156 – 2 7/8" squares

Half-square triangle units

C Match the green small squares to the neutral squares with right sides together. Slice on the diagonal from corner to corner yielding 104 matched pairs. Stitch. Press. Trim dog ears. Make 104. Units measure 2 1/2" unfinished, finishing at 2".

Wing Triangles

D Slice the remaining 104 squares from corner to corner on the diagonal to yield 208 wing triangles. Stitch a wing triangle on either side of each green half square triangle unit as shown. Press seams toward wing triangles just added. Trim dog ears. Make 104.

E Slice the 52 green large squares on the diagonal from corner to corner to yield 104 large triangles. Match a large triangle with each of the wing triangle units and stitch. Press seams toward the large triangle. Make 104. Units measure 4 1/2" unfinished, finishing at 4".

F Arrange two Fox units and two Geese units as shown to create one block quarter. Stitch. Press. Make 52. Units measure 8 1/2" unfinished, finishing at 8".

G Arrange 4 Fox and Geese blocks into one large Carolina Star block. Stitch. Press. Make 13. Blocks measure 16 1/2" unfinished, finishing at 16".

Poinsettia blocks

Make 12 – 16 1/2" unfinished, finishing at 16".

From the gold print, cut 13 – 2 1/2" strips x the width of the fabric.

From neutral scraps, cut 13 – 2 1/2" strips x the width of the fabric.

Note: The number of strips required may vary depending on the length of your scrap strips.

H Stitch neutral scrap strips to gold strips. Press to the gold print. Sub-cut strip sets into 2 1/2" sections. Make 192.

Poinsettia petals

From the red scraps, cut 192 – 2 1/2" x 4 1/2" rectangles.

From the neutral scraps cut 384 – 2 1/2" squares

I Place 1 square at the end of a red rectangle with right sides together. Stitch on the diagonal from corner to corner. Finger press seam back to make sure the triangle matches the edges of the base rectangle. If it matches, trim excess. If not, un-sew and re-sew! Repeat for all 192 rectangles. Trim Excess.

Note: you might want to draw a line on the back of the neutral squares from corner to corner to help you sew accurately. There are also many tools designed for your machine to help you stitch corner to corner in this method.

At this point you can decide if you want to save your "bonus triangles" as they are trimmed. Before trimming, I like to sew a second seam a scant 3/8" toward the corner and trim between the seams. This gives me a bonus triangle square that I can trim up to 2", which is a very useable size for me! Test your bonus square to see if you need to skinny down on the seam a bit if it turns out less than 2" in size.

Repeat for the other side of the red rectangle unit, making sure that ALL seams angle in the same direction. All of these Poinsettia Petals are identical to each other. Make 192. Units measure 2 1/2" x 4 1/2" unfinished, finishing at 2" x 4".

J Following diagram, stitch a gold/neutral unit to a Poinsettia Petal. Make 192. Units measure 4 1/2" unfinished, finishing at 4".

K Lay out 4 Poinsettia Petal units as shown to create one Poinsettia Star. Make 48. Units measure 8 1/2" unfinished, finishing at 4".

L Sew 4 Poinsettia Star blocks together into one large block. Make 12. Blocks measure 16 1/2" square, finishing at 16".

Quilt top center assembly

Referring to the Quilt Assembly Diagram on page 92, lay out the blocks. Stitch blocks into rows, joining rows to complete the quilt center.

Borders

Inner border

Your quilt center should measure 80 1/2" square before adding the inner border. The inner border is a "spacer" designed to get the pieced border to fit the quilt. Please note that if your quilt does NOT measure 80 1/2" square, you are going to have to adjust the size of the inner border to build the quilt center up to fit your pieced outer border.

From the beige stripe, cut 9 – 2 1/2" strips x the width of the fabric.

From the red, cut 4 - 2 1/2" squares.

Join the strips end to end with diagonal seams to make one long length, measuring approximately 360". Press the seams open.

Lay quilt out on the floor, smoothing it gently. Do not tug or pull. Measure the quilt through the center from top to bottom. Cut two inner side borders this length.

Repeat for top and bottom inner borders, measuring across the quilt center. Cut top and bottom borders this length.

Sew inner side borders to the quilt sides with right sides together, pinning to match centers and ends. Ease where necessary to fit. Press seams to the borders.

Add a red cornerstone to each end of both top and bottom borders. Press seams to the borders. Stitch top and bottom inner borders to quilt center, pinning to match centers and ends, easing where necessary. Press the seams to the borders.

Pieced outer border

From the red scraps, cut:
22 – 5 1/4" squares

From the neutral scraps, cut:
21 – 5 1/4" squares

From the green scraps, cut:
1 – 5 1/4" square. Cut twice diagonally with an X to yield 4 quarter-square triangle units.

40 – 4 7/8" squares. Cut diagonally from corner to corner to yield 80 half-square triangle units.

If you look closely at the quilt diagram you will see that there is a quarter-square triangle hourglass unit in the center of each border length. This is the "change direction" unit. To the left of the "change direction" unit, the border pieces are positioned one direction, and to the right, they change direction in mirror image of the others. This isn't something you can do just by rotating the unit. They have to be sewn in mirror image, so you are going to want to pay close attention to your piecing.

Match 20 red squares and 20 neutral squares with right sides together. Slice twice on the diagonal with an X to yield 80 quarter-square triangle pairs.

M As you stitch, you will sew 40 units with the red fabric on top and 40 units with the neutral fabric on top. This will give you the mirror image that you need. Press seam toward the red triangles.

N-O Add a large green triangle to each pieced quarter square unit. Make 40 of each. Units measure 4 1/2", finishing at 4".

P Cut the remaining red squares, the green square and the neutral square twice on the diagonal with an X to give the pieces required for the 4 border center units. Arrange as shown, and stitch. Press. Trim dog ears. Units measure 4 1/2" unfinished, finishing at 4".

Q Join 10 left facing border units together end to end. Make 4.

R Join 10 Right facing border units together end to end as shown. Make 4

S Add a left facing border segment and a right facing border segment to either side of a pieced quarter-square triangle unit. Make 4.

T Attach a fox unit to each end of two of the borders to complete top and bottom borders. Press.

Attaching pieced borders

Add side borders to quilt by pinning to match centers and ends. Stitch, easing where necessary to fit. Press.

Add top and bottom borders to quilt, pinning to match centers and ends. Stitch, easing where necessary to fit. Press.

Finishing

Carolina Christmas is quilted in a swirl of curls and feathers in an antique gold thread. Random lengths of 2 1/2" strips are sewn together on the diagonal for a scrappy red binding that finishes the quilt.

A

HALF-SQUARE TRIANGLE UNIT
2 1/2" square unfinished
Make 216

B

FOX UNIT
4 1/2" square unfinished
Make 108

C

HALF-SQUARE TRIANGLE UNIT
2 1/2" square unfinished
Make 104

D

WING TRIANGLE
Make 104

E

GEESE UNIT
4 1/2" square unfinished
Make 104

F
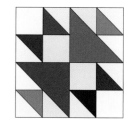

FOX AND GEESE BLOCK
8 1/2" square unfinished
Make 52

G

CAROLINA STAR
16 1/2" square unfinished
Make 13

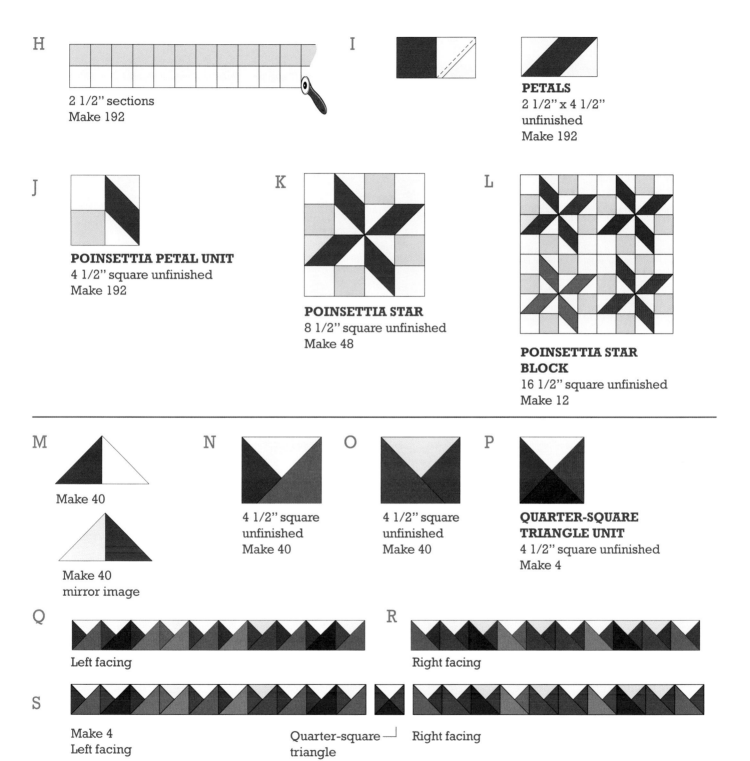

H
2 1/2" sections
Make 192

I

PETALS
2 1/2" x 4 1/2"
unfinished
Make 192

J
POINSETTIA PETAL UNIT
4 1/2" square unfinished
Make 192

K
POINSETTIA STAR
8 1/2" square unfinished
Make 48

L
**POINSETTIA STAR
BLOCK**
16 1/2" square unfinished
Make 12

M
Make 40

Make 40
mirror image

N
4 1/2" square
unfinished
Make 40

O
4 1/2" square
unfinished
Make 40

P
**QUARTER-SQUARE
TRIANGLE UNIT**
4 1/2" square unfinished
Make 4

Q
Left facing

R
Right facing

S
Make 4
Left facing

Quarter-square ⌐
triangle

Right facing

T
Make 2

ASSEMBLY DIAGRAM

On the flip side

I dug into my box of orphan blocks to make a riotously fun scrappy back for **Carolina Christmas!** It is really a two-sided quilt! I arranged the blocks in panels the length of the quilt, filling in areas with hunks and chunks of leftover Christmas fabrics. Definitely a one-of-a-kind finish!

Resources

Specialty Rulers

EZ Quilting by Wrights
help@wrights.com
Phone: (800) 660-0415
Website: www.ezquilt.com

Creative Grids USA
400 W. Dussel Dr.
Maumee, OH 43537
Phone: 419.893.3636
Website: www.creativegridsusa.com

Quilting Designs

Darlene Epp, Trillium House Designs
PO Box 1776
Sumas, WA 98295-1776
Phone: (604) 847-9500
Fax: (604) 847-9235
Email: eppd@telus.net
Website: www.trilliumhousedesigns.com

Keryn Emmerson, Kin Quilting Designs
PO Box 48 Crystal Brook SA 5523
Australia
Ph: 08 86363029 Fax: 08 8636 3054
Email: keryn@kerynemmerson.com
Website: www.kerynemmerson.com

Patricia E Ritter, Urban Elementz
125 Sunny Creek
New Braunfels, TX 78132
Phone (830) 964-6133
Email: patricia@urbanelementz.com
Website: www.urbanelementz.com

Hermoine Agee, Lorien Quilting
30 Lockwood Rd,
 Belgrave Heights 3160 VIC Australia
Phone: (03) 9754 4916
Email hermione@lorienquilting.com
Website: www.lorienquilting.com

Using Specialty Rulers

This book on making scraps quilting wouldn't be complete without listing some of my favorite tools. I am in no way affiliated with any of the companies who produce these rulers. I just love their products. There are many ruler manufacturers out there – you might find you like one kind better than another. These are a sampling of my favorites.

Note: The resources section (left) lists more information on these companies and how to access step-by-step tutorials on how to use the rulers.

6 1/2" x 12 1/2" rotary ruler by Creative Grids

I find this ruler to be the best size for just about everything. I like that there is no color other than black and white. And the lines are thin enough that I don't have to guess where the edge of my fabric is underneath that line.

Sometimes rulers have so many markings that it is hard to find just the line you need. Since my scraps are cut and sorted in 1/2 inch increments, most of the time I don't need 3/8" or 7/8" lines. And as I get older, my eyesight gets more persnickety!

Easy Square and Easy Square Jr.
by EZ Quilting

For smaller cuts I use the Easy Square Jr. It has only 1/4" markings and 1/2" markings. I like the dotted 1/4" line all the way around the square. I use this one when trimming blocks. It's great for paper piecing because I can put the dotted line on the line on the paper, and trim 1/4" past it. It's also great for cutting smaller scraps into squares and bricks without having to use a huge ruler.

The 9-1/2" Easy Square is great for squaring up larger blocks. Two sides have that 1/4" seam allowance marked so I can be sure not to trim off points.

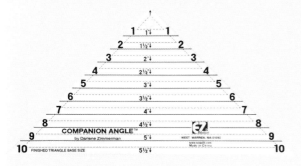

Easy Angle and Companion Angle
by EZ Quilting

I use the **Easy Angle** ruler to cut half-square triangle units from strips without having to add that 7/8" to the finished size! You just add 1/2" to the finished size of the unit to cut your strip, and the rest of the math is added in for you on the angled side. Cut matched sets with your strips right sides together and you are ready to just feed the half-square triangle pairs through your machine. This works great with my scrap strips, because I don't have that 7/8" to worry about.

The **Companion Angle**, when used with the **Easy Angle**, can make a number of units that I use most often including the "goose" part of flying geese units and "hour glass" units. It also works anywhere else I want the straight of grain to be on the longest side of the triangle. This versatile ruler also works with strips in the size I already keep on hand.

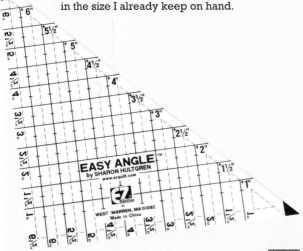

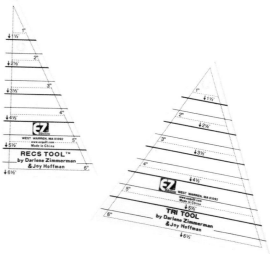

Tri Recs by EZ quilting

The Tri Recs tool gives you two for one! There is a large base triangle that becomes the background of star points, and a long skinny side triangle that becomes the star points themselves. As with the other rulers, the best part of using these is that the base triangle and the star point triangles are cut using the same sizes of strips and fit together wonderfully with great results. The rulers can also be used individually to create dogtooth borders, or split-rectangle units.

Quilts for this book were made using the following rulers:

Easy Angle
Carolina Christmas
Holy Toledo
Hawk's Nest
Criss Cross Applesauce
Goose In A Puddle
Paths & Paving Stones
Stars Over Shallotte
Smith Mountain Morning
Tumalo Trail
Old Kentucky Album (Border)

Companion Angle
Rectangle Wrangle
Old Kentucky Album (Border)
Carolina Christmas

Tri Recs
Smith Mountain Morning

Easy Square (For squaring up units)
Fair & Square
Criss Cross Applesauce

About The Author

Break the rules, think outside the box and find what brings you joy.

Bonnie K Hunter is passionate about quilting, focusing mainly on scrap quilts with the simple feeling of "making do." She started her love affair with quilting in a home economics class her senior year of high school in 1980 and has never looked back. Before quilting became her full time career, Bonnie was the owner and designer of Needle In A Haystack!! creating more than 70 patterns for dolls and stuffed animals with a country primitive feel.

Many of her designs were licensed through the Butterick Pattern Company, translated into 7 languages and sold around the globe through fabric stores. But quilting has always been Bonnie's first love. She has been machine quilting since 1989 and professionally long arm quilting for the public since 1995, retiring in 2009 when she no longer had the time due to her teaching, traveling and writing schedule. She has been featured in magazines both for her quilt patterns and articles she has written on scrap management and using that stash to its full potential.

Bonnie is dedicated to continuing the traditions of quilting. She enjoys meeting with quilters, teaching workshops and lecturing to quilt guilds all over the word, challenging quilters to break the rules, think outside the box and find what brings them joy.

When not traveling and teaching, she spends her time piecing scrap quilts, enjoying the peaceful reward of hand quilting as much as machine quilting, and loving life in her wooded surroundings in beautiful rural Wallburg, North Carolina. She and her husband, Dave, are the proud parents of two grown sons, Jason, and Jeffrey. They round out their household with Sadie the dog, and three cats – Oscar, Emmylou and Chloe – who keep Bonnie company while she designs, quilts and plays happily with her fabric.

Catch up with Bonnie's doings through her extensive website at www.Quiltville.com. You will find Quiltville's calendar for lectures and workshops, tips and tricks, technique tutorials and a long list of free quilt patterns to help you dig into your scraps. From there, head over to Quiltville.blogspot.com for Bonnie's (almost) daily blog, Quiltville's Quips & Snips. Her email list, Quiltvillechat@yahoogroups.com has become a hot spot for mystery quilters with a focus on using scraps and stash.